# PROJECT MANAGEMENT

# PROJECT MANAGEMENT

## *How to Plan and Manage Successful Projects*

# Joan Knutson and Ira Bitz

Linda S. Henderson, Ph.D.
Technical Editor

**American Management Association**

*This publication is designed to provide accurate and authoritative
information in regard to the subject matter covered. It is sold with
the understanding that the publisher is not engaged in rendering
legal, accounting, or other professional service. If legal advice or
other expert assistance is required, the services of a competent
professional person should be sought.*

*Library of Congress Cataloging-in-Publication Data*

*Knutson, Joan.*
     *Project management : how to plan and manage successful projects /
Joan Knutson and Ira Bitz  ;  Linda S. Henderson, technical editor.*
          *p.   cm.*
     *Includes bibliographical references and index.*
     *ISBN 0-8144-5043-1*
     *1.  Industrial project management   I.  Bitz, Ira.   II.  Title.*
*T56.8.K58   1991                                     90-56410*
*658.4'04—dc20                                         CIP*

*Printing number*

*10  9  8  7  6  5  4  3  2  1*

This book is dedicated to the
**American Management Association,**
which has offered us a forum for sharing our philosophies. In particular, we dedicate this book to
Vern Lautner, Division Manager, Information Systems and Technology, who has been a strong sup-
porter for over twenty years.

# Contents

# Acknowledgments

First and foremost, the authors would like to thank Dr. Linda Henderson for taking the thoughts of two crusty old project managers and turning them into communicable project management English. Also, we want to thank Muriel Rogers for the computer graphics support. Last but not least, we want to acknowledge the AMACOM staff, Myles Thompson for his role as Project Client, Jackie Laks Gorman for her developmental assistance, and Richard Gatjens and Beverly H. Miller (through Beehive Production Services) for the copy editing. We couldn't have completed this work without all of you.

# Chapter 1

# Introduction to Project Management

If you were asked to define the term *project,* what words would come to mind? *Time? Resources* (or lack of)*? One-of-a-kind effort? Deliverables or products? Complex? No authority over other groups? Budget?*

A project is a unique effort to introduce or produce a new product or service conforming to certain specifications and applicable standards. This effort is completed within the project parameters including fixed time, cost, human resources, and asset limits. Projects are said to be similar to the mating of two elephants: They start at a very high level with lots of noise and activity, but it takes forever for anything to materialize!

A more serious definition is that a project is a well-organized development of an end product that had a discrete beginning, a discrete end, and a discrete deliverable. Our goal is to help you become more organized as you work toward this objective.

Project management is the discipline that relates all of those words that you thought of that apply to *project.* This discipline cultivates the expertise to plan, monitor, track, and manage the people, the time, the budget, and the quality of the work on projects. Project management fulfills two purposes: (1) It provides the technical and business documentation to communicate the plan and, subsequently, the status that facilitates comparison of the plan against actual performance, and (2) it supports the development of the managerial skills to facilitate better management of the people and their project(s). Project management is a proactive style of management. Negotiation techniques and good communication and analytical skills are integral parts of this approach. Another key ingredient is the evaluation of performance against those objectives. Central to this management style is the application of high standards of quality to the project work.

Project management is a means by which to fit the many complex pieces of the project puzzle together. This is accomplished by dealing with both human and technical elements of the discipline of project management. Here is our definition of project management:

### Definition of Project Management

> Project management is a set of principles, methods, tools, and techniques for the effective management of objective-oriented work in the context of a specific and unique organizational environment.

The project management process encompasses these tasks:

- Assembling a project team with the expertise necessary to execute the project
- Establishing the technical objectives
- Planning the project
- Managing changes to the scope
- Controlling the undertaking so that it is completed on schedule and within budget

Project management is an evolving discipline that integrates the processes of producing the end product with the processes of planning, change management, control, and initiating preventive and corrective action. It begins when a decision is made to devote resources to an effort and ends when the desired result has been accomplished.

Project management is not designed for the management and control of nonproject, day-to-day activities within the organization. Responsibility for the day-to-day planning, operations, and control of the staff remains with the functional managers and is accomplished with existing tools and techniques. Responsibility for the technical direction of the work also remains with the functional managers. Functional management supports the project management approach rather than being a part of it. The manual and computer-based techniques used to plan and control work within functional areas can and should be used in conjunction with project management techniques. Necessarily, planning and control efforts associated with functional work will have to encompass the portions of projects to which the function must contribute and should be done in a manner that supports the project management information requirements.

## A Science and an Art

Project management is both a science and an art. It is perceived as a science because it is supported by charts, graphs, mathematical calculations, and other technical tools. Producing these charts requires the hard skills to manage a project. But project management is also driven by political, interpersonal, and organizational factors—thus the "art" of project management. Communication, negotiation, and conflict resolution are only a few of the soft skills used in the art of project management.

Each topic explored in this book provides you with both the hard and the soft skills you will need to manage your projects efficiently and effectively. This book provides you with the technical tools of project management to address the scientific side of the discipline, as well as the human behavioral techniques.

## Characteristics of Work Using Project Management

The word *project* is a buzzword. The tendency is to use it very loosely.

People refer to the jobs they have been assigned to perform as projects. The secretary refers to cleaning out a file cabinet and disposing of old, outdated material as a project. The youth refers to cleaning up his or her room as a project. A spouse refers to wallpapering the bedroom as a project. These assignments, however—and others like them—lack the characteristics that lend themselves to the application of the discipline of project management. Project management can be used with work that has three major characteristics: desired technical objectives, a deadline, and a budget (see Figure 1-1).

1. *A discrete technical objective:* If knowledge of the end product or service does not exist, it is extremely difficult to produce a plan. In this circumstance, some type of planning may be possible, but project plan-

**Figure 1-1.** Characteristics of project management.

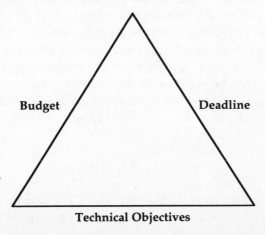

Technical Objectives

ning it is not! If the definition of the technical objective is part of the project, the effective application of project management requires that the project be broken into several smaller projects, the first of which will have the technical objective as its end product. In addition, the end product should be capable of being examined in some objective manner to determine whether it possesses the attributes and quality desired by the individual(s) for whom the project is being accomplished. If the product will be assessed on the basis of subjective criteria, it is much more difficult to plan and to manage the effort.

2. *A deadline:* The deadline can be established prior to the development of the project plan, or it can be the result of negotiation between the project manager and the client after the plan has been conceived. In either case, the project team ultimately works toward a designated end date, with some consequence associated with any delay in completion of the effort.

3. *A budget:* The budget can be in the form of dollars and/or staffing required; it can be established prior to the development of the project plan, or it can be the result of negotiations between the project manager and the client based on the plan.

In addition, the project manager and the other personnel with the requisite subject matter expertise must be able to divide or partition the work into small, discrete segments whose completion can be measured. This partitioning or decomposition of the work results in the development of a task (or to-do) list. If the task list is hierarchical and has a logical structure, it is called a work breakdown structure (WBS).

There should be an established sequence in which to perform the segments of the project. If the segments are to be performed in a random sequence, the effort still may be planned, but much of the discipline of project management does not apply. There should be a method for estimating the effort required to accomplish each component of the assignment. If significant phases of the effort cannot be estimated, the methodology of project management will not yield the desired results.

Project work obviously involves a client—the person for whom the project is being undertaken. This person or persons can be referred to as the client, the customer, the user, or the project sponsor. The client is the person who must be satisfied if the project is to be a success. In most instances, the client controls the purse strings and approves change requests made during the course of the project.

## Overview

In this book, we focus on several key project management processes and models. Chapter 2 thoroughly discusses the key questions that project managers must answer in order to initiate and define a project. A critical part of initiating and defining a project is building the project team. Chapter 3 describes the typical process used for assembling a project team and explores in detail the ways to build a strong and successful team.

The foundation of all projects is the plan. Chapters 4 and 5 provide extensive coverage of project planning. Chapter 4 addresses in depth the process for planning a project, which encompasses a five-step integrated planning model. The specific techniques of project planning are covered in Chapter 5, which describes in detail how to work through the five-step model through the use of charts, graphs, mathematical calculations, and validation techniques.

The project management environment is dynamic and constantly in flux. Chapter 6 analyzes the typical changes that take place in project baseline schedules, resource allocations, and budgets. Our analysis also includes a close look at the various sources of change to the technical objectives of the project's end product.

The effective and successful management of change requires the efficient use of project control methods. Chapter 7 thus describes a five-step model for controlling a project: updating the status, analyzing the impact, acting on variances, publishing the revisions, and informing management. Chapter 8 addresses the role of reports and reviews for controlling and reporting project status.

Determining the value of work completed on a project is the subject of Chapter 9, which addresses the major component for measuring the completion of work: assessments of the state of the project based on milestone completions. Finally, in Chapter 10, we look at ways to use software, training, and administrative support to increase the effectiveness of project management.

# Chapter 2
# Initiating a Project

A story about Gertrude Stein underscores the need for effectively initiating a project. As Stein was lying on her deathbed, surrounded by friends and followers, she was approached by a good friend, who whispered in her ear, "Gertrude, what is the ANSWER?" There was a long pause. Then Stein slowly sat upright, looked her questioner in the eye, and replied, "What is the QUESTION?"

"What is the question?" provides the overall direction for this chapter. If you don't understand the question, you cannot possibly be expected to find the solution. Nor can you plan or manage the project. Therefore, in this chapter we discuss how to initiate a project.

## Criteria for Initiating a Project

There are four criteria for initiating a project:

### B-A-N-C Criteria

> Budget
>
> Authority
>
> Need
>
> Cycle

These criteria highlight the key questions that should be asked and, ultimately, answered in any project. You may interpret these questions differently depending on your industry, its prevailing economic trends, or your organization's competitive position within the marketplace. Regardless of how strong you think your company or division is in the external/internal marketplace, misjudging business opportunities or submitting a less than high-quality proposal can lose business that is needed to grow or survive.

Let's take a close look at the key questions that need to be addressed in each of the B-A-N-C areas. First, does the client have the *budget* (funding) to pay for the job? If not, when will the funding be available? If the answer is "not in the near future," this still might be a good future project opportunity. In this case, don't put a lot of time and effort into writing a lengthy proposal, but don't lose touch with the prospect.

Second, does your contact have the *authority* to approve the project? If not, has he or she been delegated the authority? If not, how far up the line does your prospect have to go to obtain approval? If your contact is not a decision maker and does not have formal or informal power to fund the project or direct access to a decision maker, this project opportunity may not be worthy of a lot of effort now (although maybe it will later).

Third, is there an identified *need* that everyone agrees on? If not, can you help define the need? Will you and/or your client contact be able to sell the need once it is substantiated? And then, can your organization satisfy the need with your current expertise or products? If not, how much risk is there in acquiring the skills or products to fulfill the assignment without exceeding the schedule and budget? If the answers to these questions are no—indicating an unfavorable risk and reward on this venture—pass up this opportunity, but keep track of it. Once the need is truly defined and once the risk is acceptable, you want to be there to offer your services.

Fourth, regarding the *cycle,* when will the client act? Is there money left in the budget for your project? Is the money allocated for your type of project, or will it be next quarter or maybe next year until monies are made available? The further away the cycle is, the less time you want to spend now; however, when that cycle draws near, be ready to ride the wave.

## The Project Client

Do you remember the television game show "To Tell the Truth"? There were three contestants, each making the same claim (to have the same job or to have achieved the same goal, for example). A panel of celebrities posed a series of questions to the contestants and then identified the contestant they believed was telling the truth. The dramatic moment in the show came when the moderator asked the person who was telling the truth to stand up. Usually there were several false moves on the part of the contestants before the genuine one stood up, to thunderous applause.

We are often reminded of this show when we ask project managers,

"Who is your client?" There are several scenarios that may occur in a project management environment when asking, "Will the real client please stand up?" Here are three of them and some advice on how to handle each one.

### Scenario 1: An Entire Department Is the Client

Our favorite example of this scenario came from a project manager who told us that the manufacturing division of his organization was his client. Even in the face of repeated probing, he refused to alter his answer. It was definitely the manufacturing division. The manufacturing division of his company employs approximately 600 people, including three who work the graveyard shift cleaning up the tool crib.

Would it be necessary to interview each of the 600 people in order to determine the project requirements? Who would approve the project plan and be an integral part of the project's day-to-day management? Who would evaluate changes of project scope? Who would be held accountable for the success or failure of the project?

Obviously a department cannot be the client of a project. Our recommendation is to have one person or a small group be the client, accountable for the project.

### Scenario 2: There Are Multiple Clients

Sometimes several people stand up and declare themselves all as the project client. This scenario has good news and bad news. The good news is that there is interest and enthusiasm for the project since more than one person considers it advantageous to be seen as the client. The bad news is the problems posed. Who will be the arbitrator or the mediator if there is disagreement among the clients? More important, who will ultimately be accountable for the success or failure of the project? Our recommendation is to have one person or a small group led by one person be the project client, accountable for the project.

### Scenario 3: Nobody Wants to Be the Project Client

In this scenario, when the question, "Will the real project client please stand up?" is asked, no one stands up. Everyone looks at each other, waiting for someone else to accept accountability for the project. Perhaps the project is not worth doing at all. Maybe the support is not there to justify proceeding with the idea. However, if the project is required, then some of the powers that be within the organization must designate an individual or a small group to be the project client. Unless this role is clearly defined, the project client may be reluctant to allow his or her name to be put on the project paperwork or may have no intention of putting any time into the project. In order to begin to set expectations in this situation, develop a job description that goes along with this assignment. This description should clearly define the degree of involvement and the specific role that this person will play in the project from initiation to completion. Once again, our recommendation is to have one person or a small group led by one person be the project client, accountable for the project.

Where should this one person or small group come from? There are several answers (or a combination of answers) to this question, such as:

### Sources for Project Clients

- The person representing the area that has the greatest vested interest in the outcome of the project
- The person from whose budget the project is being funded
- The person who has a success record of on-time, on-budget project completions
- The person who has the political pull to get all the areas in the company to work together on the project
- The highest-level decision maker who has the clout to make things happen
- The person who wants it bad enough to put the energy into the project and make it successful
- All of the above

Keep in mind these two rules of thumb when selecting a project client or having one selected for you: (1) have one person or a small group led by one person be the project client and be accountable for the project, and (2) have that person be strong enough and dedicated enough to invest the time and energy to fulfill the role successfully.

## What Are Your Overall Objectives?

The client, once determined, must work with the project manager to establish the objectives for the project. Project objectives are variously, and loosely, defined as the scope, technical objectives, statement of work, and/or specifications. This set of terms is often misunderstood and in need of explication and clarification. Consensus on the meaning of these terms will probably never be achieved. However, some framework for their use is helpful.

### Project Objectives

*Project objectives* is the broadest and most inclusive of the terms; all project targets are part of the project objectives. Thus, the objectives are the characteristics of the deliverable(s), the target costs at completion, the target completion date, and the target resource and asset utilization at completion. Without the first three characteristics, the project objectives are incomplete; the last two are optional. The target cost at completion and the target completion date can be negotiated after preparation of the plan, or they can be provided to the project manager as constraints to the planning process.

### Technical Objectives

*Technical objectives* refers to the subset of the project objectives that addresses the characteristics of the deliverable(s). Many people use the term *scope* to refer to the technical objectives. The technical objectives contain two parts: specifications, which describe the characteristics of the product or service that is being developed in the project, and standards, which enumerate the governmental, institutional, and organizational norms that the project or service is expected to meet. We might also include the assumptions made to cover gaps in available information during planning as part of the technical objectives. These assumptions must be considered part of the project objectives and may be considered part of the technical objectives.

### Statement of Work

A *statement of work* is usually synonymous with the technical objectives of a project, but the term is applied differently by different organizations. Regardless of the terminology utilized, if the work effort is to be considered a project, the following three parameters must be met:

#### Parameters of a Project

---

1.  A statement describing the end-of-work item to be produced as a result of completing the project
2.  A stated period of performance
3.  A budget

---

Let's discuss the first parameter, which describes the end-of-work item to be produced.

## Defining Project Requirements

Defining requirements forces the project manager to define clearly and concisely the scope of the work and place parameters, or a fence, around the project before the plans are developed. When the subject of technical objectives is raised, references to the requirements of the end product or to the deliverable are often made.

The requirements are the components of the specifications of a deliverable defined by the project manager and the project client. The definition of the requirements occurs after the goal of the project has been given to the project manager but before the detailed plan for the project is created. The requirements describe the desired features or performance characteristics of the product in quantifiable terms, necessary so that the results can be measured. One of the problems with requirements is that they tend to overlap, and there is always some question as to where one begins and another leaves off. Nevertheless, overlapping should not be regarded as a disadvantage, because it tends to ensure comprehensive coverage of the desired attributes of the end product. There are a number of possible requirements for describing and measuring a deliverable:

### Requirements for Describing and Measuring a Deliverable

- Quality, performance, and quantity
- Reliability and maintainability
- Capability to survive
- Operability
- Manufacturability
- Flexibility
- Regulatory compliance
- Materials use
- Community relations and corporate image

### *Quality, Performance, and Quantity*

*Quality* is a broad and complex requirement. It can be described as excellence, robustness, or a level of perfection in the product. *Performance* is usually more specific and may also be composed of additional considerations. Performance may be measurable in terms of miles per hour or tensile strength, for example, or it can be discussed in nonmeasurable terms, such as the end users' level of satisfaction with the way a product functions. The requirement of *quantity* raises the question, When does the project end? Clearly if the objective of the project is to produce seven identical items, project management may be utilized to manage the entire effort until the seventh item has been delivered. But what if the quantity is 25,000 items to be produced over a period of several years? Should project management be used to control the production effort? Probably not. Nevertheless, a definition of completion of the project is required in order to plan for the transition from project management to production management. This definition might be the completion of a pilot manufacturing run or the point at which the bill of materials for the product is initiated in the computer. The point is to have a tangible definition.

### Reliability and Maintainability

*Reliability* is defined as mean time between failures or mean time to replacement of a component, part, subsystem, or system. It can also refer to the useful life of the product. In both cases, the desired level of reliability should be part of the definition of the objectives of the project. *Maintainability* is the mean time to repair or replace a component, part, subsystem, or system. The end product must be designed to support the level of maintainability that the end user desires. There is often an interplay between reliability and maintainability; one drives the other. Many companies trade on the reliability or maintainability of their products (e.g., the loneliness of the Maytag repairman).

### Capability to Survive

This function relates to the capability of the end-of-work product to endure in its environment. Issues like the range of temperatures and relative humidity in which the product can operate are considered to be part of survivability. In addition, the ability to transport a computer, handle it roughly, and have it operate well can be a survivability criterion.

### Operability

Is the user able to operate the product? The size of the work crew required to operate the product is part of this issue, as is the amount of training required for its successful operation. *Operability* refers to many of the issues of system or product design that are commonly known as human engineering issues. Operability is one of the areas of the project technical objectives that tend to be overlooked and can have serious implications once the product has been delivered to the end user or client.

### Manufacturability

Can the project team or the recipient of the design manufacture the product? Manufacturability has an image of smokestack industries and the fabrication of complex industrial equipment, but it is an issue in other industries as well. For example, in the area of software development, programmers need to be able to create the necessary code from the product design. In the construction industry, *manufacturability* is replaced by *structurability*. Regardless of industry type, manufacturability can and should be defined and specified.

### Flexibility

*Flexibility* generally refers to an attempt to produce an end-of-work item that has multiple applications or can be put to use in a number of areas. Modularity is related to flexibility. Building the end-of-work item from standard modules or designing it as a complex of standard modules can enable the modules to be used for other applications in the future, thereby increasing the return on investment for the project.

### Regulatory Compliance

*Regulatory compliance* refers to the international, national, state, and local or municipal regulations with which the project may have to comply. In addition, project standards may be determined by private organizations such as Underwriters Laboratories, Inc., and/or the organization performing the project. Even within an organization, corporate, divisional, and/or departmental standards may exist. All of these sources comprise the body of regulations with which the project may have to comply.

### Materials Use

A project team can often find itself constrained by the organization's preference for certain types of material. The Brick and Masonry Institute, for instance, probably would not favor a headquarters facility constructed with aluminum siding. Related requirements are packaging and product appearance.

### Community Relations and Corporate Image

Community relations is particularly important in construction project management, where concern with disruptions in the neighborhood of the construction is part of the project team's mandate. Community relations often becomes an issue in other types of projects as well, such as the installation of communications equipment that might interfere with television reception or the installation of high-voltage power lines that could cause environmental damage. Corporate image, a more global concern, can affect the packaging of products, serve as the basis for the approval or killing of certain projects, or affect materials use.

Project requirements serve as the basis upon which the plan is built.

Part of the challenge to project teams is to make sure that all of the requirements have been identified prior to submitting a project plan. The result will be a better plan, with fewer errors of omission during the course of the project. The requirements should be quantified in order to measure the project team's performance. Let's take a look at two examples and decide what is wrong with the way the project requirement is stated:

1. *"The new system must be better than anything we have used in the past."* What does *better* mean? What is the standard-of-performance criterion that will equate itself to "better" after the project is complete? Do we have a standard-of-performance criterion for current productivity against which we can compare future productivity after the system is installed?

2. *"You have to understand that this will be the greatest thing since sliced white bread, and our company cannot survive without it."* This explains the why, not the what. Although it is essential that the project client and manager understand the why, the what must be defined.

Documenting the answers to these questions in the form of a proposal or business case sets the stage for the remainder of the project. It requires a concentrated, sustained effort. However, the return on investment for the time and effort spent will be significant.

## Conducting Focused Interviews With the Project Client

In order to understand and to document the project requirements and objectives, you as project manager need to interview the project client to determine what belongs within the scope of the project, what work needs to be done, when the end product is needed, who needs to be involved, and any additional considerations. Here are some questions to ask the project client:

### Determining the Client's Objectives

- What do you really want?
- Is there a specific time when you need it? What circumstances have mandated this time frame?
- What are the exclusions, if any (for example, the new product will not be sold outside the United States)? What specifications do not have to be included in this project?
- By what standard will you measure the end product?
- How do you see the end product performing?
- What will be the use(s) for the end product?

### Creating a Context for the Project

- Why do you want the project done?
- Why now?
- What have you tried before, and what were the results?
- What are the risks?
- What do you foresee as the impact that this product will have in your organization and in the marketplace?
- Are there any future implications that should be considered in addition to the short-term benefits?
- What will it cost?
- What are the tangible and intangible benefits to be realized?

## Preparing the Project Initiation Documentation

Among the topics that may be addressed in the documentation for initiating a project, some are mandatory, and others are optional. Depending on the size of the project, its visibility, and the requirements of management or the client, select the segments that provide the best return for the effort expended.

- *Problem/opportunity statement* (mandatory): What is the problem or opportunity that this project addresses? This section should provide background on the factors that led to this project and, where appropriate, some history of what has been attempted in the past.

- *Scope definition* (mandatory): What are the quantifiable characteristics or end results to be achieved? The scope definition should respond to the problem or to the opportunity. The end product might be a specified product, process, or service.

- *Completion criteria* (mandatory): What needs to be done? How will it be measured in the most objective terms? How will we know when we're finished? The completion criteria should indicate whether it is the design, the prototype, or a complete working product, system, or process that is the goal. Consequently, this completion criterion or standard of performance needs to be quantifiable. The objective is to eliminate subjective analysis after the completion of the project.

- *Assumptions* (optional): What has been assumed? Is everyone aware of these assumptions? Remember that what you, the project manager, assume will form the basis upon which to build the project plans. If the other people on the team, particularly the client, have not made the same assumptions, there will be a major variance in expectations.

- *Impact statement and interfaces* (optional): Upon whom or what will this project have an impact or an interface? Most projects do not exist in a vacuum. The creation of their end products may have a ripple effect within the organization, outside the organization, or both. These impacts may have either a beneficial or detrimental effect, so they should be documented and evaluated.

- *Risks* (optional): What are the risks of doing or not doing this project? One variation of risk analysis can be a detailed mathematical presentation with which to project the financial and other ramifications. Another variation is to provide a business analysis of the major risks and rewards that provide the basis for deciding whether it is prudent to proceed with the project.

- *Resource requirements* (optional): What resources will be required? This section should alert particular areas of the organization that their staff members will be required to support this project. You may also want to announce whether you will need any special or unusual resources for the project. Do not make definitive specifications at this point since you do not have enough information to plan. Rather, include a generic statement of skill mixes that will be eventually requested.

- *Constraints* (optional): Are there any special constraints imposed upon the project? These could be environmental factors such as terrain, weather conditions, or Environmental Protection Agency requirements. There may be constraints imposed by equipment, technology, or chronological limitations to be considered. Get them out on the table at the beginning of the project so that you will have the opportunity to reevaluate and pursue alternative solutions.

# Chapter 3
# Building the Project Team

Building the project team is your primary and most critical task. Your success is based on choosing the right team members and obtaining their commitment to the project. In this chapter we describe the typical process for assembling a project team, explore in detail the ways to build a strong and successful project team, and discuss the factors that affect a team's performance during the course of the project.

## Assembling the Project Team

Typically, you should begin assembling a project team while developing the work breakdown structure (WBS) for the project because that is when the skills required to execute the project become apparent. Assess the ability of your permanently assigned staff to fill the project requirements. If there are required skills that they do not have, identify other sources of personnel possessing these skills.

Once you have identified these sources, begin your negotiations to assemble the project team. Approach each supervisor of personnel with the required skills and explain the nature of the project and the assignment. If you can't obtain a commitment from the supervisor to support the project, investigate alternative sources or raise the problem with senior management in order to get assistance in obtaining the required commitment. Even after the individual in question has been assigned to your team, you may need to conduct subsequent negotiations with the person's supervisor. For example, the project might call for the participation of multiple members of the skill group on the project, or it might require a long-term commitment of a key member of the group.

The organization's structure and distribution of authority will affect the nature of these negotiations. In some cases, you may find it necessary to alter the project's schedule and budget to accommodate the availability of the staff you need. In other situations, the skill group manager may find it necessary to alter other priorities to accommodate the demands of the project. In either case, after the negotiations are completed, the head of the skill group will be asked to assign specific staff members to accommodate the project plan. Nevertheless, if you are still unable to obtain specific assignments to the plan from the supervisor, you may have to investigate alternative sources of the required skill or go to senior management for a decision on the relative priority of the project versus other components of the skill group's workload.

There are a variety of objective or technical criteria to use in choosing the team members: perceived technical ability, estimating proficiency, project management skills, experience as a task leader on other projects, and attitude toward this project and toward projects in general. Often it is the subjective or personal attributes that are critical—for example, prior experience with the subject matter, information from fellow project managers, or an opinion based on casual contact with the individual offered as a team member. For these and similar reasons, we suggest that you talk to potential team members before negotiating to have them join the project. In order to determine the potential effectiveness of prospective team members, you need answers to the following key questions:

### What to Look for in Prospective Team Members

1. Would I want this individual working for me?
2. Would I want this individual as one of my peers?
3. Would I want to work for this individual?

## Defining and Documenting Team Member Commitment

In order to obtain commitment from team members, it is important to define and document their contributions to the team. Two tools can help you here: the skills inventory matrix and the responsibility matrix.

### Skills Inventory Matrix

Every project requires a variety of skills that will need to be matched to the appropriate tasks. In the beginning of the project, it is important that you appropriately match people, skills, and tasks. As the project progresses, it may be necessary to split assignments, add staff to existing assignments, or trade assignments. In order to have this flexibility, you need to know which people on the project team possess which skills. In many cases, you will already have this information.

If you want to codify an inventory of the skills available from your project team, we suggest using or adapting the skills inventory matrix shown in Figure 3-1. Set up a simple matrix form with the skills or areas

**Figure 3-1.** Skills inventory matrix by area of expertise.

| | PROGRAMMER 1 | PROGRAMMER 2 | PROGRAMMER 3 | ANALYST 1 | ANALYST 2 | TECHNICAL WRITER | TRAINING | QUALITY ASSURANCE | USER | PROJECT LEADER |
|------|---|---|---|---|---|---|---|---|---|---|
| Joan | | | X | X | | X | | | | X |
| Seth | | | | | | | | | X | |
| Guy | X | | | | | | | X | | |
| Bob | | X | X | | | | | X | | |
| Jean | | | | | X | | | | | |
| Marie | | | | | X | X | X | | | |

of expertise depicted along the x-axis and the resources (people) along the y-axis. Then place a checkmark in the box indicating which skill(s) each team member possesses. In this way, you create a useful overview of team members and skills from which to assign tasks.

### Responsibility Matrix

Now consider who on the project team is most qualified to perform each task. In order to do this, develop a responsibility matrix (Figure 3-2). This matrix is the documentation of a performance contract among the project manager, the project team members, and their supervisors. It is an important mechanism for obtaining individual commitment, or buy-in, and for graphically depicting that responsibility.

To develop the matrix, list the tasks on the left axis and the names or job titles of the project team members along the top. Then match the tasks to the members by indicating the person with prime responsibility (P) and those having support responsibility (S). Each task requires one and only one prime; several supporting team members may be assigned. The team member with prime responsibility is accountable for ensuring that the task comes in on time, within budget, and at the expected level of quality. Those in a support capacity are chosen because they have skills needed on that task. Follow these five rules of thumb when preparing a responsibility matrix:

#### Preparing a Responsibility Matrix

1. Assign staff because they have the correct skills, not because they have time available.
2. Do not assign too many people to one task.
3. Obtain buy-in from team members: "ask," don't "tell."
4. Consider who is good at what, who wants to do what, who can or cannot work together, and who likes to create versus maintain.
5. From the perspective of the project, consider what skills are needed, what skills are available, and, if someone left a task, whether his or her work could be redistributed.

Ideally, as the project manager, you have some exposure to these areas of responsibility. This background—coupled with intuition, a bit of psychology, and a bit of luck—can make the task of assigning responsibility both challenging and rewarding.

**Figure 3-2.** Responsibility matrix.

| PROJECT NAME | | PREPARED BY | | | | PAGE | OF |
|---|---|---|---|---|---|---|---|
| Install Purchased Package | | J. Ryan | | | | 1 | 1 |

PROJECT MANAGER: J. Ryan

LEGEND:
P = Prime
S = Support

## RESPONSIBILITY MATRIX

| TASK ID | TASK | Joan R. | Bob S. | Guy R. | Marie S. | Jean M. | Seth K. |
|---|---|---|---|---|---|---|---|
| A | Assess Requirements | P | S | S | S | S | S |
| B | Design Business System | S | P | S | S |  | S |
| C | Modify Purchased Package |  |  | P |  | S |  |
| D | Modify In-House Procedures | S | S |  | P | S | S |
| E | Modify Manual Systems Flow |  | P |  | S | S |  |
| F | Test Purchased Package | S |  | P |  | S | S |
| G | Test In-House Procedures | S |  |  | P | S | S |
| H | Test Manual Systems Flow | S | P |  | S | S | S |
| I | Implement New Software Package | P | S | S | S | S | S |
| J | Train Staff |  |  |  | P |  |  |

## Building a Strong Project Team

A strong team is the nucleus of and can ensure the success of a project. The team members are asked to deal with specified constraints of time and dollars, sometimes under great stress. As project manager, you need to give them your technical guidance, your management expertise, plus a significant intangible—your enthusiasm and support. In this section we consider the techniques for developing a strong project team, the importance of building a team communication plan, and your responsibility to, accountability for, and authority over the project team.

### *Techniques for Team Development*

We recommend that you consider using five techniques to build a solid foundation for coordinating your project team's work efforts.

1. *Build a broad-based team.* Choose the best people available to play on your team. By *best,* we don't just mean people who bring a diverse set of skills, experience, and personalities to your project; we mean people who are known to get the job done and are team players. Familiarize yourself with their strengths and weaknesses, both technical and emotional, by observing and listening and by asking their boss, other project managers who have worked with them, and others with whom they have worked in the past about their abilities. Evaluate each person's comments, but make your own judgment. (Of course, sometimes we are not given the choice but are told who will be assigned to our projects.)

2. *Establish a formal leader.* Note the adjectives before the word *leader: a* and *formal. A* means singular. Project team members cannot divide their loyalty and responsibility among different captains. As project manager, you must be the only person running the project. *Formal* means that you have been officially delegated the job of captain with the responsibility and authority that comes with it. Make sure that everyone on the team understands your role, who assigned you this role, why it is necessary to have a single point of control, and how you plan to exercise your authority.

3. *Build and maintain team spirit.* If you become apathetic, your team will become apathetic too. You don't have to share negative developments with the team. If it does not affect a team member's ability to perform the job successfully, keep the downside to yourself. That is part of your leadership role. Also, if you are not a rah-rah leader, don't pretend. You can still impart a sense of professionalism and urgency without it. However, you might want to find someone on the team to be the cheerleader for you—the person who sets up the milestone party or the Friday beer bust. Well-timed and -deserved thanks can go a long way.

4. *Elicit management support.* In many organizations, project managers are dependent upon personnel who are not members of their staff for the performance of project tasks. Usually these team members have been assigned by their managers or supervisors to the project for the duration of it or for the time required to perform a specific task or group of tasks.

The assignment of these persons to the project presents you with a unique challenge: to obtain a commitment to the project from the assigned team members, to motivate them to achieve the project goals in a timely and cost-effective manner, and to influence them to identify with the team and its objective. To meet this challenge, you need to be skilled in persuasion, motivational techniques, leadership techniques, and the use of influence in the absence of line authority. Even these skills will not ensure your success, however. The team member, for example, may be a reluctant participant in the project, viewing it as an interruption of his or her normal duties.

One means of increasing the probability of success for the project is to convince each team member that the project is an essential part of his or her job. This convincing must be done by the team members' supervisor or manager, however, not by you. It is easier to convince the team member of the importance of the assignment if the person's supervisor agrees that you will have something to say in the person's performance appraisal.

5. *Keep team members informed.* Nothing is more frustrating to project team members than changing the game plan without their knowledge. As project manager, you need the respect of the team. You can build this respect in part by establishing communication channels so that you and the team members can exchange information in a timely and accurate way.

## Building a Team Communication Plan

Some team members need to be aware of the project status more frequently than others; some may need to provide functional input on a regular basis; and some will have varying needs for information by virtue of their role on tasks (whether prime or support). As project manager, you need to define your goals for team communication during the early stage of the team's formation and determine the forms of communication you will use with each person on the team: meetings (group and/or individual), telephone calls, written status reports, electronic mail, or some combination of these.

If you plan to use written communication, define the content, level of detail, and format for the reports. Keep in mind that your written communication will be most effective if you report to the needs of each audience. Work this out in advance so you're sure that you will hit the mark.

If you plan to use meetings, devise a strategy that identifies who will attend, how often meetings will be held and where, when they will be scheduled, and who will be responsible for agendas, minutes, and other logistics. Your team meeting plan should be part of your project plan so that everyone involved will know how and when meetings will take place.

Whether you plan formal or informal communication with your team, consider how often you will be in touch. Some members will need or request more frequent communication than others. In addition to regularly scheduled communication, you may plan meetings or reports around key project milestones or other checkpoints. In general, the following guidelines are useful to your communication plan:

### Guidelines for Developing Effective Team Communication

---

- Involve key members of your project team in developing a communication plan.
- Work with each team member to define how and when your communication will take place and how you'll work together to solve problems that might arise on the project.
- Devise a strategy with each team member to help ensure that information does not fall through a crack and to prevent ruffled feathers that often occur when messages are miscommunicated or omitted.
- Begin developing your communication plan as soon as you take on a new project, and update it as needed. Players often change in the project universe. Develop new communication strategies when this happens. Newcomers or replacement project team members are often left out in the cold and cannot fully contribute unless you take time to involve them.

---

There is one key communication skill that you as project manager need to develop and use: listening. The power of this communication tool cannot be overestimated for it leads to several important outcomes for the project: increased productivity and quality of work, improved job satisfaction, and a clearer sense of roles and expectations. Let's look at the key verbal and nonverbal behaviors for active listening.

#### *Verbal Listening Behaviors*

- *Ask questions* to clarify or to gather information on the topic. Make your questions more than just closed-ended ones that require only a yes or no response. Make them probing and constructive. Don't be too embarrassed to say, "I didn't understand you. Would you please say that in another way so that I can understand."

- *Paraphrase* what the speaker has said. In some situations, you and the speaker come from different parts of the organization and may be using different terminologies. If something is said to you in unfamiliar jargon, paraphrase the information in words that are meaningful to you.
- *Summarize at certain intervals* what the speaker has said. Periodically confirm that you have understood and are on the same wavelength with the speaker by restating (concisely, please) what you have heard up to this point.
- *Ask the speaker for examples.* If the statement is not clear, an example or a visual impression of the subject can help clarify the information. Asking for an analogy (some description similar to the topic at hand) might lead to shared understanding.
- *Ascertain the speaker's feelings* and acknowledge them (for example, "You sound pretty frustrated by the whole thing"). There are times within the conversation when the speaker just needs to get something off his or her chest. Regard this discussion as important to the speaker. If it has relevance to your relationship with the speaker or to the project, deal with it. If the speaker's feelings are irrelevant to the topic or to the welfare of the project, explain that you recognize the importance of what is being said, but the speaker should readdress the issue with a more appropriate listener.

### Nonverbal Listening Behaviors

- *Make eye contact* with the speaker. To some people, eye contact indicates honesty, straightforwardness, and openness. If you are unwilling to look someone straight in the eye when talking, you are not creating the attention, connection, or personal bond that is necessary and meaningful for good communication.
- *Be expressive.* An alert, interested expression motivates the speaker to be open. If you only appear to be interested, the speaker will probably sense your lack of enthusiasm.
- *Move close to the speaker.* The intimacy allows you to establish a more friendly, constructive communication. We once watched a fine negotiator interact with people whom he knew quite well. Each time someone made a comment that lended to our friend's position, he physically shifted his chair closer to that person's chair. If someone said something contrary to his position, he shifted his chair away from the speaker. It soon became a game to see how much someone could say that reflected this man's thinking and therefore how close he would move his chair to those in agreement.

Later, several of the people got into the game and started moving their chairs in the same manner.

- *Listen for the intent* of what the speaker is trying to communicate. The message is not only what the person is saying but how it is being said. Remember "read between the lines"? We must be willing to listen between the words.

You get out of listening only what you put into it. Project team members may be telling you something important. They may be indicating that the project will come in six months late or that the budget is going to be overrun by 190 percent. In some cases, the message is not obvious. Perhaps they are expressing frustration in getting part of the job completed, which may be indicative of a global problem. Your team members need your help.

Listening is probably the best communication skill. Pay attention, don't interrupt, don't change the subject, and don't take over. Make every person with whom you interact feel that what he or she is saying is the most important thing in your life at that moment and that it will influence the outcome of the project. Remember that each communication may have a significant impact on some aspect of your project. Don't miss that vital message.

A project team communication plan has many benefits: you'll have fewer forgotten tasks if you remember to involve the right people early enough in the project to guide your planning efforts, and you're likely to reduce the number of wrenches thrown at the project midstream. Perhaps the strongest benefits are on the human side of the equation: You're likely to achieve greater buy-in to the project, and you may even reduce the impact of difficult people as well.

## The Project Manager's Authority

One of the biggest concerns of most project managers is their high degree of responsibility—for managing the project management process and delivering a high-quality end product or service—coupled with a limited authority to manage team members and other resources. As a project manager, how can you acquire authority? Let's explore the possible answers to this question by distinguishing between informal and formal authority.

**Informal authority** flows from any of the following sources:

- *Experience/knowledge authority:* This refers to knowing more about a specific subject than anyone else. This authority is tenuous, however; a new contender can be coming up to take this venerable position.
- *Authority by association:* This is the power of who you know. But it

lasts only as long as the "who you know" status is intact and the association with this person is perceived as strong.

- *Personality-based authority:* Well-placed prior favors or accommodations may be returned when they provide the most results. Team members don't forget that time when you were flexible on a deadline or when you made other concessions they needed. Some people call this "calling-in markers." We call it the golden rule of doing good business.
- *Credibility authority:* This type of authority differs from experience, knowledge, and technical qualifications. It is gained by the manner in which you conduct yourself: being honest, fair, and responsible to the organization, to the team, and to yourself.

**Formal authority** comes from any of the following sources:

- *Direct line authority:* You are the person to whom the people on the team report directly. You may have hired them and may have the ability to fire, and in all cases you determine their raises, their promotions, and their future growth within the organization. Most project managers, however, do not have line authority over their project team members.
- *Job title or position within the organizational hierarchy:* Job title and/or position do not in and of themselves guarantee authority, but they certainly do position one to command the attention of others.
- *Pecuniary authority:* This is power over the purse strings—probably the most effective control that a project manager can have. If you have control over the budget, then you have control over the project. This is particularly true if you have the option to employ internal staff, recruit new staff, or use outside contractors. You may also be given the authority to provide financial incentives to your most productive team members.
- *Mandated authority:* A senior executive mandates that everyone will cooperate with the project manager. This delegated power, however, is only as strong as the executive who issues the mandate. It is also only as strong as the consistent backing that this sponsor provides to the project manager. The sponsor may give the greatest kick-off speech in the world, but without his or her continued support, this power erodes very quickly.
- *Performance appraisal review authority:* With this type of authority, you have input into team members' performance appraisals. This power is only as effective as the degree of influence that this information has on team members' raises and promotions.

Let's look more closely at this last type of authority: input to a team member's performance appraisal review. Some organizations have an organizational policy that governs the manner in which the project manager provides performance information to the team member's manager or supervisor. Some of the essential elements of this process follow:

### How to Provide Performance Feedback

- Project team members should know from the start of an assignment that their manager or supervisor will obtain and use performance appraisal information from you.
- The assignment must be for a sufficient number of person-hours to warrant invoking the process.
- Your input should be obtained when the performance of the team member is fresh in your mind rather than at the end of the appraisal period.
- Anything critical you have to say about the performance of the team member should be reviewed with him or her before the end of the appraisal period.
- The team member's manager or supervisor should use this information as part of the team member's overall performance review.

### *Attaining and Using Power*

Authority, formal and informal, is rarely permanent. It must be constantly earned and re-earned. Rather than think about the formal authority that you do not have, plan to acquire the power that you need to achieve your goals.

The word *power* has two important meanings to you in your role as project manager. First is the rational meaning: the ability to get things done. In an organization, this usually means the ability to get other people to do work, especially in service of the organization's goals. Second is the nonrational meaning: people's feelings and emotional needs that relate to being in control. Many people have strong emotional needs to be in control of others or to avoid being controlled by others. Most of us have strong needs to be recognized, acknowledged, and respected by others.

Emotional needs are easily stirred up when one person is trying to get another to do something. It is easy for individuals to start out trying to accomplish a project goal through others and then to get confused between the organization's needs and their own emotional need for control or recognition. It's also easy for the other person to get confused over the same issues. When this happens, we often refer to the interaction as politics, a power struggle, or a personality conflict.

One of the reasons it is so easy to get into this sort of struggle is that human needs for control and recognition are often unconscious, and consequently reactions are unplanned. We don't need to become amateur psychologists to be good project managers, but it can be very useful to take a few minutes to identify some key power needs we are likely to have to deal with as project managers. This can help us later to avoid getting confused and will also give us bargaining power when we need it. We can gain power through the use of several strategies.

### Influencing

Influencing uses a strategy of shared power. It assumes that both parties have equal power in their own areas and that no bargaining or pressuring needs to take place. Instead, influencing relies on interpersonal skills to get others to cooperate for common goals. Influencing others can be accomplished by following two guidelines:

### Requirements for Influencing

1. Build and maintain reliability by being consistent in what you ask for and what you do, following through on commitments, and being clear abut how a decision will be made.
2. Use a flexible interpersonal style in which you adjust to the person you're with, especially your voice tone and nonverbal behaviors.

In the long run, influencing is the most practical strategy for project managers to use. It is low cost and effective regardless of one's formal level of authority, and it's good politics. Sometimes you may feel your influencing skills aren't quite up to the task, or perhaps you have used them but the other party isn't following through. Then you may wish to move on to the next strategy.

### Negotiating

Negotiating uses a strategy of trading for power. It assumes that each person has something the other wants, and neither will yield it unless compensated. Before negotiating, you have to do some analysis. First, determine what the other person wants, either through asking outright or possibly doing some shrewd guesswork. Second, identify what you have (or can get) that others want. Finally, identify your own needs in the situation. What specifically do you want? What is it worth to you? Do your own personal needs and wants conflict with the other party's? Once you have finished analyzing the situation, you're ready to negotiate with the other person. The following skills will serve you well in this process:

### Key Skills and Behaviors for Negotiating Successfully

- Differentiate between wants and needs—both theirs and yours.
- Ask high, and offer low—but don't be ridiculous.
- When you make a concession, act as if you are yielding something of value; don't just give in.
- Always make sure both parties feel as if they have won. This is win-win negotiating. Never let the other party leave feeling as if he or she has been taken.

Negotiating is a useful fallback strategy when you're dealing with a tough customer and feel there's a high risk of not getting what you need. Some people make an entire life-style of negotiating and become very good at it.

If you feel you are facing a situation that is too critical to risk negotiating or if you have negotiated and the other party isn't honoring his or her side of the bargain, you may decide to move on to the next strategy.

### *Using Coercion*

Coercion uses a strategy of power imposition. It assumes that the other person has something you want but will yield it only under force. It turns to formal organizational lines of authority to issue orders and get compliance and requires that you know (or find out) answers to the following questions:

- Who "owns" the project? Usually it is the client. If the original client is no longer there and no owner is apparent, who is answerable to the organization for business results that this project supports?
- Is there anyone else at a high enough level who is championing the project or has become visibly connected with it? This person's authority is the lever you will use to get compliance.
- Who has formal authority over the person whose compliance you need?

Your job is easiest if the person whose compliance you need is under the client's lines of authority. If not, the client will have to solve the same set of problems you have just been trying to solve: how to get his peer to exert authority over the person whose compliance you need. It is worth noting that the client will have the same set of strategies to choose from: influencing, negotiating, and using coercion. An important political consideration is how far up the owner's line of authority you want to go to make your request. A general rule is to go to the lowest level you can and still be reasonably sure of success.

Once you have identified the lever of authority, you still need to persuade him or her to act. In some cases, a word may be enough, but generally you will need negotiating skills. It is also wise to have standard project status report documentation, showing where the project is now and the likely consequences if no action is taken.

Using coercion is generally the least practical and most politically expensive strategy to use. Sometimes it is necessary to use, but it should be your last resort, not your first move.

Each of the three strategies has been presented in a pure form in order to give a clear explanation. In reality, they are mixed together according to your personal style and the needs of the situation. The more flexible you are in using and mixing the strategies, the more powerful you are likely to be in motivating others.

## Managing the Team During the Project

As work progresses on a project, several external factors will undoubtedly have an effect on the team's performance. In this section, we will discuss four of these factors: poor performers, turnover, adding resources, and overtime.

### Poor Performers

All projects are not blessed with superstars. In fact, many projects are not even blessed with average performers. Not only are poor performers nonproductive, but they also distract and drag down good performers around them. How can you get rid of poor performance?

First, find out if the poor performers are competent. Perhaps these people are wrong for the project tasks assigned; they may perform more effectively if assigned to another task. Then determine whether these people are aware that they are perceived as poor performers. If they are not, performance feedback and/or counseling may help them improve their performance. If neither reassignment nor counseling helps, you must remove poor performers from the project if possible. If that is not politically feasible, then isolate these people so they cause a minimal amount of negative influence on the rest of the team.

### Turnover

Turnover during the project can cause a negative impact on the team. If the project loses a team member and introduces a replacement, time and effort are necessary to orient that new team member. The effect on the productivity of the team depends on the point at which the turnover occurred and the role of the person who has left the team. Turnover that occurs late in the project will have the greatest negative impact. Other team members are too engrossed at this point to have the time to work with the new team members, who have a great deal to absorb in order to be productive. In addition, studies indicate that loss of the project manager or the client will have the greatest effect on the capability of the project team to bring the project in on time and within budget. Worthy of note is that the secretary or administrative assistant has the greatest impact on the team after the project manager and the client.

Functional managers or supervisors should be required (other than in emergencies) to give advance notice to you of their intent to replace a team member so you have the opportunity to evaluate the impact in advance of the actual transfer. If you take exception to the transfer, raise the issue with the manager or supervisor. If agreement cannot be reached, you have the option of escalating the issue to an arbitrator or mediator who, after examining priorities and impacts, will determine the appropriate course of action. This must be done prior to the transfer; reversal of an implemented decision is often difficult and sometimes impossible.

Not all decisions will favor you. Additionally, the longer and larger the project is, the more likely it is that transfers will compromise your team's ability to meet the project targets. You can deal with these roadblocks by requesting a contingency, set aside to deal with the added cost and lost time of assimilating new team members throughout the project.

The key issue here is not the relative expertise of the original team member and the replacement; it is the commitment, motivation, and the sense of ownership of the plan. Thus, you may take exception to transfers even when you realize they are more experienced and productive employees than the original team member.

Three guidelines will help you deal with turnover:

1. If you can orchestrate turnover, accomplish it early in the project.
2. If the person being moved is the project manager or client, expect a significant impact.
3. If there is turnover, immediately reevaluate and renegotiate the time and budget required to complete the project.

### Adding Human Resources

Adding people to the team will have an impact on the productivity of the team as a whole. There is a law of diminishing returns when adding personnel onto the project team: adding one more person may reduce the time, adding another person may further reduce the time, but somewhere in the progression of adding additional resources, the time will increase. Frederick Brooks, in his book *The Mythical Man-Month*, suggests that this phenomenon occurs because the addition of new personnel requires additional communication channels that must be established and maintained.[1] Brooks puts forth this formula:

$$I = \frac{E\,(E-1)}{2},$$

where $I$ is the number of interfaces or communication channels that must be established and $E$ is the number of elements or people on the project team. For example, if there are ten elements or people on the project team, forty-five communication channels must be established (Figure 3-3). If you add one more person to the team, there will now be eleven people on the team and fifty-five required communication channels.

Obviously there is a point beyond which the introduction of additional resources to the project is nonproductive rather than productive. The number of interactions is significant, and it can have a profound impact on the total number of person-hours necessary to perform the task. When you plan tasks that have more than one person assigned to them, take into account the number of potential interactions.

### Effect of Overtime

There are two major philosophies concerning overtime: (1) overtime is ineffective, and (2) overtime is effective only when it is required for short intervals. This latter philosophy suggests that project team members are willing to rise to the occasion and accept overtime under two conditions: they see the end of the overtime, and they understand why it is necessary. When overtime becomes a way of life, it is no longer effective or productive. Here's an interesting example.

In his book *Advanced Project Management*, F L Harrison suggests that a person who works 6 days at 12 hours per day (72 person-hours) is approximately 88 percent productive.[2] In effect, he would give the

---

[1] *The Mythical Man-Month: Essays on Software Engineering* (Reading, Mass.: Addison-Wesley Pub. Co., 1982).
[2] *Advanced Project Management*, 2nd ed. (New York: John Wiley & Sons, 1985).

**Figure 3-3.** Adding resources to a project.

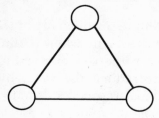

## 3 Elements
## 3 Potential Interactions

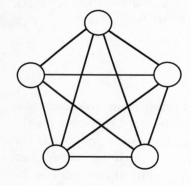

## 5 Elements
## 10 Potential Interactions

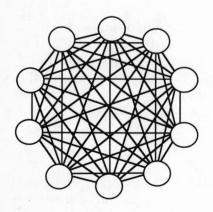

## 10 Elements
## 45 Potential Interactions

$$I = \frac{E\,(E - 1)}{2}$$

project 72 × 88 percent = 63.4 effective effort hours. If, however, this person works 7 days at 12 hours per day (84 person-hours), he would be only 77 percent productive and provide the project with 64.7 effective effort hours (84 × 77 percent = 64.7). By working an extra 12-hour day, he would provide the project with only an additional 1.3 hours of effective effort. Whether you agree with these percentages of productivity or not, we believe that you will agree with the premise: people who work too much consecutive overtime show diminished productivity.

# Chapter 4
# A Model for Project Planning

This is the first of two chapters that deal with the development of the project plan. In this chapter, we focus on the process of planning and address the general procedures for planning project schedules, resources, dollars, and work accomplishment. In Chapter 5, we explain in detail the specific tools and techniques necessary for using these procedures.

## The Integrated Project Plan

An integrated project plan is the primary tool for effective coordination of project work. It consists of separate schedule, cost, human resource, capital asset, and achievement subplans. These subplans are integrated through the use of a common work breakdown structure. The objectives of the project plan are to:

- Determine and portray the scope of effort required in order to fulfill the project objectives.
- Identify all personnel responsible for performance of work on the project.
- Schedule the required work (tasks) and establish a timetable.
- Indicate the human resources and capital assets necessary for each task.
- Determine the budget for each component of the work task or group of tasks.

This integrated project plan facilitates communication among senior management, the project manager, the functional managers, the project team, and any contractor(s). The plan is designed to facilitate project coordination, communication, planning, and control rather than to provide technical direction to the participants. There are eight key considerations for developing integrated project plans.

### How to Develop Integrated Project Plans

1. Involve personnel assigned to the team in planning at the earliest possible moment.
2. Involve team members continuously until the plan is completed and approved.
3. Avoid being too optimistic or too pessimistic in estimating. The desired estimate has a high probability of realization. Ideally, there should be a 50 percent probability of either being over or under the estimate.
4. Negotiate work commitments from project team members who work for functional managers outside your authority.
5. Obtain commitments for all effort (human resources, equipment, and assets required to perform the work) in the work breakdown structure.
6. Obtain a written commitment to project plans from all parties.
7. Remember that an integrated project plan is a step-by-step process. Each step builds on what has been accomplished in previous steps. Avoid alterations to the planning sequence since they may reduce participant commitment to the plan.
8. Understand that the effort required to develop the integrated project plan depends on the project's clarity, realism, objectives, size, scope, and complexity; the team's experience, cooperation, and enthusiasm; and continuous, visible, and strong support by management for the project management process.

The act of listing tasks in a schedule or collecting costs in a cost report does not constitute project planning. *Project planning is a disciplined process supporting the coordination and direction of resources such as time, people, and dollars to achieve product and project parameters established by management.* It emphasizes the process of planning the work required to produce the project's end product rather than focusing on the technical aspects necessary to produce the product. You must answer these five essential questions during project planning:

### Essential Questions to Ask During Project Planning

*What (technical objectives):* The question of what is to be accomplished is addressed through the review of the technical objectives by the project manager and the team.

*How (work breakdown structure):* The technical objectives are achieved by developing a work breakdown structure, which is a checklist of tasks that must be performed.

*Who (resource commitment and utilization plan):* The issue of who will perform the work is addressed, and the organizational units responsible for components of the work are incorporated into the work breakdown structure at the appropriate level of detail.

*When (schedule):* Further into the planning process, the questions of how long each element of work will take, when it will be performed, and what resources and assets will be used in its performance are addressed.

*How much (budget):* How much will it cost to perform the project?

An integrated project plan contains the data that support the what, how, who, when, and how much of a project. Several benefits are realized from this integration:

1. Effective communication is encouraged within the team and to the project client and management.
2. A final check is provided for ensuring that the project objectives are attainable with the time and resources available.
3. An integrated plan establishes the scope and a level of responsibility and authority for all team members and their respective work efforts.
4. The plan serves as the basis for analyzing, negotiating, and recording scope changes and commitments of time, personnel, and dollars to the project. In this way, a baseline is formed for measuring progress, calculating variances, and determining preventive or corrective actions.
5. The plan minimizes the need for narrative reporting. Comparisons of the plan against actual performance in the form of lists or graphics make reporting more efficient and effective. In this way, it can provide an audit trail and a documentation of changes that can remind team members and the client why changes were made during the evolution of the project.
6. It records, in a standard format, critical project data that can be used in planning future projects.

## The Five-Step Planning Model

An integrated project plan maximizes the probability of achieving the project objectives through five major work steps:

### The Five-Step Planning Model

1. Define the project.
2. Model the project.
3. Estimate and schedule the project.
4. Balance the plan.
5. Approve and publish the plan.

### Step 1: Define the Project

As discussed in Chapter 2, once you have reviewed the objectives and accepted the assignment, you must follow a sequence of planning steps to ensure that an adequate plan will result. There is some overlap between the start of planning and the process of developing and approving the project objectives. Early in the planning process, the project objectives will have been thoroughly reviewed and approved by management. Then a decision to proceed with plan development will be made.

Acceptance of the assignment by the project manager is generally assumed. Sometimes, however, you may determine that it is in the best interests of the organization for you to refuse the assignment. You may doubt that the technical objectives are attainable or believe that the project cannot be accomplished within the budget and schedule. You should bring these concerns to the attention of management. A project manager's refusal to take the assignment commonly causes renegotiation of the objectives rather than rejection of the project. There may be an alteration of the technical objectives of the assignment, the schedule, or the cost objectives. If you do not believe that you possess the requisite technical expertise to manage the undertaking, refusing the assignment is also acceptable. In this case, a more technically strong individual may be assigned to assist you.

You are well advised to perform a personal review of the adequacy of the specifications and list of applicable standards for the end product or service. Evaluate whether there have been any external influences or regulatory changes during the period between the formulation of the objectives and the start of the project that might necessitate a change in the objectives. As a result of this personal assessment, you can indicate that there is a satisfactory basis for developing the plan or initiate a process of clarification and modification of the project objectives. At the conclusion of this effort, the objectives are either modified to address your concerns or the project is terminated prior to plan development.

As project manager, you will serve as the integrative force throughout the project, and it is your responsibility to establish and maintain project files that all team members will use during the project. The files should include all original and revised project plans, all milestone products, relevant studies or research results, the statement of objectives, status reports, and project correspondence. Upon completion of a project, the files (often referred to as the project notebook) should be reviewed. After selective disposal of papers that are no longer relevant, the files should be archived for future project managers to refer to. It is important not to discard work breakdown structures and networks from old projects since the next assignment might repeat significant portions.

### Step 2: Model the Project

Modeling focuses on developing a simulation of the effort required to achieve the project objectives. The model produces two deliverables: the *work breakdown structure* (WBS), which determines all the work efforts required to bring the project to a successful completion, and the *network,* a sequence in which the tasks should be performed.

The WBS is a framework in which to define the work tasks for the project. The work tasks are arranged in a hierarchy of major categories (or phases) of work. Each category is then broken down into lower levels of detail that describe the specific tasks necessary to complete the major categories of work. (We discuss the details for developing these categories and work tasks in Chapter 5.)

Developing a WBS requires the contributions of the project team members. An effective method for developing a WBS is to hold a group session where team members can freely brainstorm and discuss their ideas. If a meeting is not feasible, interview team members one at a time or send out questionnaires. Keep in mind, however, that a group session will always produce the best results. (At the end of this chapter, we discuss in more detail how to set up and facilitate team meetings.)

Once the WBS has been completed, the team can develop a network showing the interrelationships among the tasks. These interrelationships, or dependencies that the tasks have with one another, are typically referred to as the relationship a predecessor task(s) has to a successor task(s). The relationship is determined by the necessity of a predecessor task to be complete (or partially complete) before the successor task can begin; that is, the start of the successor task is dependent on (or constrained by) the predecessor task. (We cover the mechanics of developing a network in the next chapter.)

### Step 3: Estimate and Schedule the Project

Estimating and scheduling focus on determining the duration, required level of funding, and required level of resources for the project. Approaches to estimating are personal. Each individual has his or her own techniques for developing an estimate of the effort required to perform a task and duration to complete the task. Some organizations have estimating procedures for use by the team, but most do not, so teams typically are left to their own devices to develop the task estimates, and the project manager is provided with minimal guidance for review and confirmation of estimates.

Most estimators begin by estimating the person-hours required to perform a task. This number becomes the basis for an estimate of elapsed time. Next is the determination of direct costs; these are the person-hours multiplied by the charge-out rate of that grade of personnel. Finally, when capital assets are required to perform the task, the type and cost to the project are determined. Estimating is a seven-step process:

## Estimating Steps

A. Develop the task estimates.
B. Process the data into a preliminary plan.
C. Compare the preliminary plan to objectives.
D. Negotiate revisions to the estimates.
E. Negotiate revisions to the project objectives.
F. Make a go/no-go decision.
G. Prepare schedules and budget.

### Step A: Develop the Task Estimates

The estimating data must be developed by the team members who are responsible for performing the work. This ensures that estimates are realistic, that there is a commitment to the estimates by the team members, and that the team will be motivated to meet the estimates. All estimates must first be processed into a preliminary plan in which each task has a planned starting date and a planned duration. The team members furnish the following data to you as project manager: the amount of time necessary to perform the work or effort of a task; the amount of calendar time or elapsed workdays necessary to complete the work tasks; capital assets by unit of measure to perform the task (e.g., purchase of equipment, special construction of facilities); and direct costs by category to perform the task (e.g., labor and materials).

The most accurate estimates result when small increments of work are being estimated. A large or complex task should be divided into subtasks for estimating, which can then be summed to the task estimate. Tasks can be performed by varying numbers of persons, depending on the nature of the work and the manner in which it is divided among the people involved. The team member should estimate each task based on the most efficient number of persons needed to execute the effort. Later the estimate can be modified to deal with the schedule or resource problems.

In preparing estimates, team members should take into account nonproductive time. This downtime factor can be based on the judgment of the estimator or can be a guideline from the functional manager. Given the nature of their work, downtime varies from unit to unit. Since projects do not constitute the entire workload of most functional units, persons assigned to a project must be expected to be diverted from time to time to deal with functional work. This nonproject loss factor should be used in developing estimates for elapsed time. These diversions do not affect the project budget, since time spent on other activities is not charged to the project. The impact on the schedule, however, must be accounted for in the estimates.

### Step B: Process the Data Into a Preliminary Plan

The preliminary project plan consists of a schedule derived from the dependency relationships and the task estimates. This schedule is prepared on a time-scale calendar chart showing when tasks are to begin, how long they will take, and when they are planned to end.

The cost budget for the project can be produced by analyzing the tasks being performed during each unit of time and dollars being spent for capital assets and direct costs. (The mechanics of how to produce the schedule and budget are discussed in the next chapter.)

### Step C: Compare the Preliminary Plan to Objectives

If only a technical objective has been established, cost and schedule are now negotiated by you with senior management. In most cases, the project objectives are determined by senior management and the client before the project is assigned to you. The technical objectives are a constant. They are the same for the schedule and budget established by senior management and for the preliminary project plan you and your team established. The comparison undertaken is (1) between the completion date established by senior management and the planned completion date, and (2) between the senior management budget and the planned cost.

If the comparisons are within a reasonable range of each other, there is no need to perform the remaining subtasks. Negotiations are not necessary when the plan incorporates the commitments of the team and meets the expectations of senior management. If the comparison is unfavorable, you must proceed to Steps D, E, and F.

If senior management did not establish a due date for the project and/or a maximum cost, then proceed directly to Step F and negotiate this with senior management. If the comparison is unfavorable because senior management has allowed too much time or too high a budget for the technical objectives, you may proceed directly to Step F and negotiate a reduction in the funding and an earlier anticipated delivery date for the project. Step E in the estimating process is performed only if the preliminary project plan exceeds the expectations of senior management.

### Step D: Negotiate Revisions to the Estimates

This step is performed if the preliminary project plan exceeds the senior management's and client's schedule and cost objectives. Perhaps senior management has established the objectives based on incomplete information or an out-of-date historical model. Regardless of the cause of the problem, you must attempt to reconcile the plan and the objectives through negotiation.

You may feel that the path of least resistance is to ask the client and senior management for additional time and funds for the project. But be aware that it is not considered appropriate to make these requests until the plan has been thoroughly reviewed and it has been determined that there are no excesses in it. Usually some facets of the plan can be modified, and some change in the schedule and cost targets is possible.

The organization needs to be committed to realistic cost and schedule objectives. However, there are dangers in negotiating estimate revisions, since considerable effort has been exerted to ensure that the project team is committed to the estimates and motivated to adhere to them. The negotiation of revisions can cause the team to lose this commitment and motivation. The result may be a set of estimates indicating that the project can be completed by the due date and within the budget but that the team does not see as credible. Therefore, use caution in the negotiations. Make sure that the members of the team do not alter the estimates in a manner that renders them impossible to achieve. (We discuss different types of negotiated revisions in the next chapter.)

### Step E: Negotiate Revisions to the Project Objectives

This step is a result of one of two sets of circumstances: (1) You approach the client and senior management for the first time in order to negotiate a schedule deadline and a budget because these were not established when the project was initiated, or, more commonly, (2) you realize there is an incompatibility between the preliminary plan and the project objectives that cannot be eliminated by negotiating estimate revisions (Step D).

In the first case, when you approach the client and senior management for the first time, the negotiations should be simple and straightforward. Present the plan for senior management's reaction and determination of whether the time frame and cost are consistent with corporate objectives. This results in an immediate move to Step F, the go/no-go decision.

In the latter case, the negotiations are more complex. Assuming that Step E is being undertaken because the objectives do not include sufficient time and/or funds for the project, there are four alternatives for management to consider:

1. *Alter the schedule and cost objectives,* so that you have sufficient time and funds to accomplish the work. You will have to assure management that the revision results in a project that is economically viable and will produce an acceptable return on investment (ROI). (This alternative will not be acceptable in the absence of such a return, unless the situation is one in which an external requirement or regulatory requirement is being fulfilled by the project and cannot be fulfilled in a more cost-effective manner.)

2. *Develop a reduced set of technical objectives* that can be accomplished within the time and funding limitations established by senior management. If you recommend this approach, senior management will seek assurances that the proposed product will nevertheless meet market expectations and provide an acceptable ROI.

3. *Implement a combination of the first two alternatives.* Recommend a modest increase in time and funding, coupled with a small reduction in the technical objectives. If you recommend this solution, management will want the same assurances as in alternatives 1 and 2 above.

4. *Cancel the project.* If you believe that the ROI cannot be increased to become attractive or that the product will fail to meet market expectations, this recommendation is the best choice. Management will seek assurance that all approaches to achieving the objectives have been explored before approving cancellation.

Regardless of the alternative you recommend and senior management decides on, there are only two acceptable outcomes to this process: (1) a plan acceptable to you, the project team, the client, and senior management or (2) cancellation of the project. There is one other possibility, however—one that we do not encourage: taking on the project on a best-efforts basis, without changing the project objectives. This approach only postpones the time when the true cost or time needed to complete the project must become a concern of senior management.

If Step E is being undertaken because the project objectives include an overabundant amount of time and/or funds, there are thee alternatives:

1. Senior management might reduce the time and budget, with provisions for contingency plans. They will want assurances that the funds taken from the project will not be required later.
2. The technical objectives could be adjusted at no increase in the time and funds allocated. Management will want assurances that any added scope will not cause schedule or cost problems later in the project.
3. Senior management might attempt a combination of the first two alternatives: a modest decrease in time and funding coupled with a smaller increase in the technical objectives. If you recommend this, senior management will want the same assurances.

Regardless of the alternative you recommend and senior management adopts, there is only one acceptable outcome: a plan acceptable to you, your team, the client, and senior management. The other possibility—a best-efforts approach to the project—does not apply in this situation.

### Step F: Make a Go/No-Go Decision

A management review should be conducted when the plan is completed. The scope is evaluated to confirm that the appropriate product will be produced, and the cost, schedule, and resource allocations are reviewed to ensure that they fall within the project boundaries. Then the plan is revised as required. There is a possibility of a no-go decision at this time if the costs are considered excessive in relation to the projected benefits, if the resources will not be available, or if the project does not fit in with management's strategic goals and objectives.

### Step G: Prepare Schedules and Budget

The preliminary plans developed in Step B can now be finalized. These final plans consist of three report documents: a schedule (which portrays when each task begins, its duration, and its end date on a time-scale calendar), a resource utilization chart (which indicates the allocation of each team member or pool of team members per unit of time), and a project budget in the form of a spread sheet or graphic representation. We thoroughly explore the techniques required for producing these documents in the next chapter.

## Step 4: Balance the Plan

Balancing is the most challenging stage in developing the plan. Balancing limited resources of the plan should occur within the project and against other project and nonproject efforts. Projects compete with each other and with nonproject work for two scarce commodities: human resources and funding. The typical organization lacks sufficient staff to perform all project and nonproject work approved by senior management and sufficient funds to perform all needed work. For these reasons, balancing is critical.

Frequently organizations apportion their funds so that approved projects are adequately funded. A lesser number of organizations allocate human resources by dividing the staff into pools or groups, one of which is available for projects. But regardless of how the allocation between project and nonproject work is made, individual projects compete for the limited human resources and funding available. The priority of the projects influences balancing. Before balancing between projects can occur, there is a need for balancing within each project.

Balancing a single project can help to ensure that its personnel demands do not exceed the organization's capacity. Time-phased resource and asset utilization plans can be laid out in tables or graphs and can be produced by project management software packages. If a team member is overcommitted, then you as project manager (in conjunction with the functional manager when necessary) need to analyze the reason for the overcommitment and to resolve the problem by using resource balancing (leveling) techniques.

In an organization with a significant project workload, management of resource supply versus demand is a key concern. Some resources are elastic in that supply can be readily increased to meet demand. Others are nonelastic and a significant lead time and/or cost is necessary to increase supply in order to meet the demand. Supply versus demand reporting should be performed for both elastic and nonelastic resources. When there is a significant difference between supply and demand, balancing, or leveling, is performed.

Resource leveling requires knowledge of anticipated supply and demand. Supply is typically determined by looking at the current size of the resource pool available and projecting changes to that pool over the period of the forecast. Demand is calculated by adding the requirements of all approved projects to the nonproject workload of the organization. Supply and demand are examined over a period of months, and periods of underutilization and overutilization of resource pools can be identified. Resource leveling occurs with the attempt to reduce demand during a period of forecasted overutilization or to increase demand during a period of forecasted underutilization. (We illustrate the details of leveling in the next chapter.)

Once individual project balancing has occurred, project needs are balanced with those of previously approved projects. Multiproject balancing can be performed manually, although the amount of data to be manipulated makes it complex and time-consuming. Balancing can be automated by delegating the decision making to a computer algorithm. The most effective approach may be computer-assisted balancing, where management utilizes the software as a decision support tool to achieve the required balance. Multiproject reports, based on the entire workload of the organization unit, are produced to support this step. Omission of any component of the workload from the reports renders the entire process meaningless. Several components of these data are the responsibility of the functional managers (e.g., the percentage of time allocated for administrative activity, nonproject activity, and vacations).

### Step 5: Approve and Publish the Plan

At this point, a document recording the plan targets (target completion date, target cost, target resource utilization, and target asset utilization) and the objective maxima (latest completion date, maximum cost, maximum resource utilization, and maximum asset utilization) should be prepared. This is the agreement among the project manager, the project client, senior management, and functional managers (where appropriate) and serves as a basis for negotiating changes in scope during the project, as well as measuring the team's performance. These agreements should be signed by the appropriate parties and distributed. Keep in mind, though, that this stage of the planning process cannot begin until balancing is complete.

Obtaining commitments for project funding is a complex undertaking. When projects extend beyond one fiscal year, obtaining a commitment for the total funds required may be impossible. In many organizations, funding commitments are made on an annual basis. Where the availability of funds has been determined during the balancing stage, securing the fund commitment should be a formality. If difficulties arise in this effort, revisiting Step 4 may be required.

In essence, obtaining commitment is the acid test of your performance in developing an integrated plan. If the process has been followed exactly, obtaining functional manager commitments to the plan is a pro forma exercise since their ability to make the commitments has been determined in the balancing stage, and any resource problems have been resolved. However, if you have not adhered to the planning process, the functional managers will refuse to commit to the resource plans, and you will have to repeat portions of the planning process. The formality of placing the functional manager's signature on a commitment sheet, to be used as a cover sheet for the plan, should be all that is involved in this step.

Similarly, obtaining senior management approval should be a pro forma exercise. Management has already reviewed the plan, and now, more than likely, they want to determine if the functional managers' commitments have been obtained before signing the cover sheet. Since quality assurance is a major thrust of management, the plan may be checked to ensure that there are adequate reviews of milestones for the end products. Once senior management has approved the plan, changes to the plan must be managed. (This is discussed in Chapter 6.)

The final step in the planning process is distribution of the integrated plan to the team, management, and other interested parties. The schedule, resource, asset, cost, and achievement plans should be graphic in nature for effective communication. Typically, work on the project begins during the planning process because many projects have extremely tight schedules. But once the plan is completed, the team begins working from it rather than on an ad hoc basis.

## Strategic Planning

In order to implement the five-step planning model, a strategy for managing the conceptual versus detailed planning is necessary. **Conceptual planning** is usually referred to as top-down planning, whereas **detailed planning** is referred to as bottom-up planning. Most organizations do both. However, when a top-down plan is prepared and presented to the client, who then accepts it, the project parameters of schedule, resource requirements, and budget are often set in concrete. Often when the bottom-up plan is completed, it does not match the committed parameters stated in the top-down plan.

### Top-Down and Bottom-Up Planning

Top-down (or conceptual) planning begins with the development of the project's technical objectives. The technical objectives may be very detailed, or they may simply identify the major characteristics of the product anticipated from the project. Top-down planning includes the development of a preliminary work breakdown structure, which is not completed until later, during bottom-up planning. Once the major work tasks in the WBS have been identified, estimates that are based on intuition or historical data are prepared and then used to assemble the top-level project plan.

Bottom-up (or detailed) planning also begins with the development of a set of technical objectives for the project; however, the technical objectives must be very detailed. Bottom-up planning also includes the development of WBS. The WBS is completed down to the level of detail for each task that must be performed in order to achieve the project objectives. Then estimates are assembled, from the bottom up, by the members of the project team. Finally, the detailed project plan is assembled from the estimates.

Let's work with an example. In Figure 4-1, the need or requirement for the work to be performed is illustrated in the triangle. This triangle can be used to characterize the results of top-down and bottom-up

**Figure 4-1.** Effort required to achieve the project objectives.

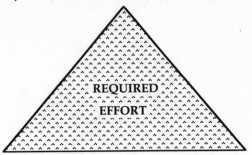

planning. After the client has developed a scope for the project, a partial WBS is formulated, presenting major elements of the effort required. Then a cost and schedule objective for the project is established, from the top down, based on the partial WBS and a host of factors external to the project, such as competitors' faster time-to-market rates. Figure 4-2 shows what can happen if only top-down planning is done. In this case, the WBS is only partial and does not contain all of the tasks needed at a level of greater detail. The resulting project coverage, provided by the WBS and estimate, contains no work that is irrelevant, but it may fail to contain certain elements of work essential to meeting the project's technical objectives.

If the idea for the project is transmitted to the project manager and team without the benefit of top-down planning, there may be a lack of direction on the project. Figure 4-3 shows what can happen if the project manager elects to prepare only a bottom-up plan. All of the detailed elements of the work have been identified, but included with them are a number of elements of work that are not essential to deliver the technical objectives of the project. In addition, there is no strategic hierarchy of planning elements, an oversight that will affect the manner in which the project is controlled. The cost and schedule objective for the effort includes these unnecessary elements of work.

A combination of top-down and bottom-up planning will produce a radically different and much improved result. After a top-down plan has been prepared, giving the project strategic direction and focus, and perhaps after the effort has been approved, a detailed, bottom-up plan is completed. This planning effort begins with the partial WBS prepared in the top-down planning effort. Then the WBS is fleshed out, and bottom-up estimates are prepared for each work element. The result is a focused plan (Figure 4-4) in which top-down planning provides the strategic focus, and bottom-up planning provides the detailed coverage. In order to assemble a project plan that is thorough and contains all of the elements of work necessary to meet the project objectives, but without containing unnecessary work, both top-down and bottom-up planning

**Figure 4-2.** Effort covered in the top-down plan.

**Figure 4-3.** Effort covered in the bottom-up plan.

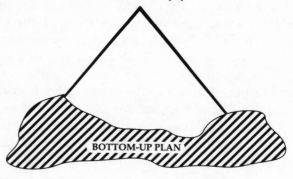

**Figure 4-4.** Effort covered in a combination of top-down and bottom-up plans.

are necessary. The two approaches complement each other and yield a plan that is most likely to reflect the true requirements of the project.

There is a potential problem with the combined use of top-down and bottom-up planning, however. Often top-down planning is used as the basis for seeking project approval. The schedule and budget developed as part of the top-down planning process are presented to senior management and/or the client to obtain their approval for the expenditure of funds on the project. This is convenient and makes economic sense, because the cost of developing the top-down plan is significantly less than that of the more detailed, bottom-up plan. But if the top-down plan is used as the basis for obtaining funding, there is no guarantee that the funding or time frame approved for the project will be adequate until *after* the detailed, bottom-up plan has been completed. We know of several instances in which there has been a considerable discrepancy between the totals of the top-down plan and the totals of the bottom-up plan. How can this problem be avoided? The answer is quite straightforward: by employing a rolling wave (or phased) approach to project planning.

### A Rolling Wave Approach to Planning

How often have you been asked for estimates of the duration and cost of a project before thoroughly understanding the scope and objectives of the effort that will be required? How often have you been correct? Although assured that these estimates were only rough figures, how often were these top-down planning figures set in concrete, never to change? What can be done to structure a more realistic alternative? Consider an analogy.

You are an expert mountain climber standing at the bottom of an imposing mountain you have never seen before. It is your job to climb this mountain and reach the bottom on the other side. The person who is funding your expedition asks, "How long will it take to get to the other side of the mountain, and how much money do you need?" Your thought processes are, "How do I know how long it is going to take to get to the other side or how much money it will cost? I have never seen this mountain before."

Would an "I don't know" answer be satisfactory to your client? Probably not. You were hired because you are an expert mountain climber and are expected to produce reasonable answers. If you shoot from the hip, the accuracy of your guess will be suspect, and sooner or later you will have to confront your error. This is top-down planning at its worst. There is no time to produce a bottom-up plan, but you know you will be held accountable to the commitments made in the top-down planning process. You seem to be caught in a lose-lose situation. Is there an alternative?

Consider the rolling wave approach illustrated in Figure 4-5. At the beginning of the wave, or climb (using the mountain climber analogy), you are standing at the bottom of the mountain with minimal knowledge of what is confronting you. But with your mountain climbing background and experience, combined with historic data gathered from other people who have tried to climb this mountain, you approximate the time and resources required. Note that the term is *approximate*, not *estimate*. This approximation should be presented in a way that provides you with as much flexibility as possible. For example: It will take six to nine weeks to

**Figure 4-5.** Rolling wave approach.

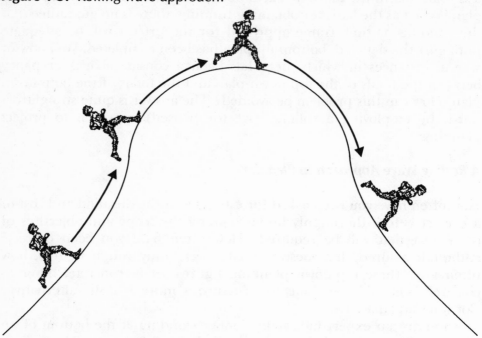

climb the mountain, require ten to twelve people, and cost about $50,000, plus or minus 15 percent. These are your top-down estimates. Because you are giving yourself room to alter your approximations over the life cycle of the project, this approach suggests that the planning process rolls out detailed plans for the foreseeable future and, as the project evolves, periodically reevaluates the schedule and budget developed in the top-down planning process.

Simultaneously, provide the project client with a plan detailing everything required to prepare the party to start moving up the mountain. Consider determining the necessary equipment, pinpointing the right people, acquiring and studying information about this particular mountain, and plotting a route. This is called *scheduling through the first planning horizon*. A planning horizon is described as planning out as far as you can see. The target may be stated as number of days, the next phase of the project, or when the next major milestone is reached. Up to this point, you have provided the client with a top-down plan of the time and resources necessary to finish the total effort and a detailed estimate for the first planning horizon.

Now the benefits of rolling wave come into effect. In the mountain climbing analogy, once the equipment and people required to make the climb have been selected and the route is mapped, planning the next phase begins. This step, which is to acquire the resources and prepare for the start of the climb, is relatively easy. Furthermore, the approximation of time and resources at this stage can be refined with a higher level of accuracy and greater confidence. At each subsequent reevaluation, the projections of the final deadline and dollars become more realistic. Eventually enough information will become available and the scope and objectives well enough defined to prepare a bottom-up detailed plan for the remainder of the project. You control using the detailed plan established for the first planning horizon. At the end of each phase, many unknowns have been resolved, and many decisions have been made.

## Saving Time and Funds With Historical Files

Over time, many projects bear a striking resemblance to others your organization has previously executed. The planning process that we have described thus far is "from scratch"; we have used no historical data from prior projects. When relevant historical data exist, planning can be accomplished more quickly and more cheaply. A central repository for files coupled with expertise in the approach to project management is a valuable asset.

Historical files, however, can be a two-edged sword. They can provide marvelous benefits; but if history is used extensively and the members of the team do not participate in the review and modification of the historical data being used, the team may lose a sense of ownership, commitment, and motivation. Moreover, there is a tendency when using unedited history to repeat bad performance since the historical data may have failed to set objectives correctly in the first place. The team must edit all historical data.

Even if there are no relevant historical data, the development of an integrated project plan may not be completely from scratch. An organization that has a product development methodology or cycle can use it as a generic work breakdown structure. Keep in mind, however, that every phase, task, and milestone included in a generic work breakdown structure is not required on every project. The team must edit the generic model much as they would edit a historical project of a similar nature in order to develop a sound plan with meaningful commitments.

## Facilitating the Project Planning Process

It is probably obvious by now that one of your key roles as project manager is to facilitate the project planning process. You must produce a schedule plan, organize functional representatives into a workable and effective project team (we use the term *organize* to indicate that a project team is created not by magic but by the use of consciously employed consideration and concentration), and prepare the project team for postplanning roles and responsibilities.

"To facilitate" means to make something easier. In the case of the planning process, it means to ease the use of project management tools in the building of a project team. Facilitating is leading others through a process, sometimes referred to as indirect training, that culminates in the development of concrete deliverables. The objective is to assist project team members in working through the planning process in order to develop the schedule, resource plan, and budget.

The facilitation process requires you to elicit or draw information from the team. To accomplish this, you must put team members at ease. The team members should know who is on the team and why, what will be expected of them in meetings, and that you will guide them through the process. This facilitation is best accomplished through private meetings with each team member in advance of the first team meeting.

Project communication meetings are integral to the planning model. The number and length of these meetings will vary according to the size and complexity of the project, as well as the level of knowledge that team members bring to the project. For some projects, the sequence of communication meetings necessary to produce the project plan may be quite short—perhaps even a few hours. For others, significant amounts of time between meetings may be required for team members to develop additional data and levels of work detail. In other words, adapt the following agenda of team communication meetings to your own situation.

### Meeting 1: Orient and Prepare the Project Team

You need to reach agreement on the objectives of the planning process with the team and demonstrate your capacity and willingness to help. Therefore, the objective of the first project communication meeting is to define the roles of team members, describe the project goals and the function of the communication meetings, and discuss how you will achieve these goals. It is important that you involve the team members in determining the agenda for future meetings so that they will attend these meetings and support the planning process.

### Meeting 2: Develop Objectives, Scope, and Work Breakdown Structure

Prior to this second meeting, provide team members with a clear statement of goals for the meeting, appropriate reading materials, and assignments. The reading materials should include the business case that initially justified the project (if one had been created), a statement of work defining the goals and objectives of the project, and the proposed first level of the WBS. Team members should be requested to review the business case and project goals and objectives, to document their role in meeting the objectives, and to isolate the first level of work effort in which they see themselves involved and develop a second level of their work breakdown.

The meeting itself addresses the project objectives and goals. They should be discussed openly by the team, with comments and questions thoroughly addressed. The scope of the project is the next item. At this point, you or the facilitator focuses on the specific elements that are a part of the project and those items that have been excluded.

The meeting then proceeds to a discussion of the strategy for meeting project objectives. In each project, there are a number of ways in which the objectives can be achieved. The facilitator elicits information relating to the strategy from members of the project team.

A discussion of restrictions and risks associated with the project follows. Here the facilitator presents such items as budgetary constraints, restrictions relating to conditions in the marketplace, and any other circumstances that affect the manner in which the project work is to progress. If the project is to have a series of go/no-go decision check-points, the facilitator discusses these points, with a complete description, if feasible, of the factors and the criteria used to make each go/no-go decision. All of the assumptions that have been made previously are presented and discussed with the project team. This is also the appropriate time to initiate a discussion of the course of action that might be appropriate if a particular assumption proves to be unfounded.

Finally, quality assurance, financial philosophy, priority of this project, and change control can be briefly discussed. This effort concludes the positioning of the project and provides for a strong foundation upon which the project plans can now be built.

### Meeting 3: Develop Final Work Breakdown Structure and Team Organization

The third meeting addresses the scope definition and reconfirms the agreement on the end product. Any areas of disagreement should be addressed immediately. Agreement on the project scope will facilitate the development of the WBS. Since the scope and the first two levels of the WBS represent the conceptual plan, they provide the direction for the balance of the WBS development.

The facilitator explains the top levels of the work breakdown structure with the team and then works with the members to reach agreement on level 2, which is detailed tasks. Small subgroups are then created with two assignments: to generate a level 3 subtask list and to determine the person (or department) who will become the task owner.

The entire project team reconvenes and reviews each level 3 subtask list for clarity and appropriateness, buys in to the responsibility assignment of the person (or group) accountable, expands the responsibility matrix to incorporate those people (groups) who will support the task owner on each task, details the deliverable(s) with a standard-of-performance criteria upon which it will be measured, and finally logs any assumptions, constraints, or risks associated with each task.

### Meeting 4: Develop Dependencies and Durations

Each task activity in the work breakdown structure, except for those that start at a fixed time, depends on a predecessor activity. We have found that the most stimulating and productive way to determine the sequence of tasks based on their dependencies is to use pad notes attached to a wall. The team writes each task on a gummed slip, places the slips on a wall, and then moves them around in order to determine the paths of their sequential and concurrent order from the start of the project to the finish.

The next team effort, time estimating, may be done in this meeting or as an assignment. If the team decides to tackle this task now, the facilitator asks interested and knowledgeable team members how much time it will take to complete each task. If the estimates are close and agreement can be reached, the estimate is recorded on the task's gummed slip. If there is a wide divergence and agreement cannot be reached, give the task owner the assignment to break the task into further subtasks and rethink the estimate. Upon receiving this more precise time estimate, go to the people supporting the task and obtain concurrence of the estimate before proceeding further.

The meeting is completed by a discussion of what comes next. The facilitator reviews the actions generated during the meeting, which include the sequence of dependency relationships and who is responsible for each task, as well as a timetable for completion.

### Meeting 5: Produce a Schedule

The team now has enough information to develop a schedule showing when tasks need to begin and end in relation to one another on a calendar. Problems with the schedule plan should be identified and assigned to individual members to resolve at this meeting. Those responsible for the critical path activities must evaluate their assignments and create contingency plans for areas of high risk. There may be other deliverables created as products of the planning process (for example, a resource loading chart or a budget). Any or all of these items may be necessary to monitor and control the project. (We discuss them in more detail in the following chapter.)

It is also important to facilitate an understanding of each deliverable with the team. We suggest that team members keep a list of open items that must be resolved prior to the next meeting and then decide who will resolve and complete each one. As a result of these types of actions, teams begin to see project progress and develop positive feelings about the process and team relationship.

In this final meeting, the facilitator discusses what is next in the planning process—for example, how data will be produced on schedule charts, if and how resource allocation will be performed, how status will be tracked, and when status meetings will be held.

## Effective Planning

The process of plan development is designed to produce documents that represent the true expectations of the team. The plan represents commitments on their part, makes a statement of the team members' ownership, and represents time frames and budgets with a high probability of being achieved. There are seven requirements for effective planning:

### Requirements for Effective Planning

1. *Parameters:* Establish parameters of quality, time, resource allocations, and cost for every project. Ensure that these parameters are realistic.
2. *Plan:* Develop a plan that will accommodate the parameters committed to.
3. *Simplicity:* Keep project plans, procedures, and reports direct, clear, and concise.
4. *Approvals:* Secure formal and informal approval of project plans.
5. *Accuracy:* Confirm that everything you disseminate is accurate.
6. *Authority and responsibility:* Place authority and responsibility in parity with what your expectations are from the project team members.
7. *Project team members:* Remember that human factors are of overriding importance.

The process of planning is critical to the success of project management. Frequently organizations have produced the correct plan documents but have failed to execute a significant percentage of the projects according to the plans. This happens when the process used to produce the plans is defective and the plans cannot be achieved. The planning documents do not accurately reflect what the project team expects to happen and do not represent commitments on the part of individuals who are motivated to realize the desired results.

# Chapter 5
# Project Planning Techniques: Schedule, Cost, and Resource Utilization

This is the second of two chapters that deal with the development of the project plan. The project objectives have already been defined in the previous chapter. Detailed project planning is now required. In this chapter, we focus on the following techniques used in planning: work breakdown structure, project network, estimating, critical path analysis, and scheduling. We then discuss how these planning techniques can be used in making important business decisions regarding mandatory target dates, resource leveling, project budget, and risk assessment and contingency planning.

## Work Breakdown Structure

The work breakdown structure (WBS) is a checklist of every activity that must be performed to create the end product. This checklist becomes the foundation for the schedule, resource allocation, and budget plans.

Create a WBS using one or more of the following methods: questionnaire, one-on-one personal interviews, or group sessions. We recommend the group sessions as the vehicle for developing the most comprehensive work breakdown structure.

Figure 5-1 shows the basic framework for a WBS. Begin its construction by isolating the major work assignments for your project. The key question the team needs to answer is, "What major work assignments must be accomplished to complete this project?" The major work assignments should be the significant chunks of work necessary to see the project through from start to finish. If you are using some type of systems or product development life cycle, your major work assignments will follow directly from the phases or stages of this life cycle.

Write each work assignment on a separate sheet of flipchart paper.

(The flipcharts give everyone an opportunity to see what has been discussed and what might have been omitted. They make returning to any previously discussed section to make further recommendations much easier.) Figure 5-2 shows the beginning of a sample work breakdown structure for a hypothetical project to install a new software package. In order to install the new package, five major work assignments must be accomplished: assess requirements, design, develop, test, and implement.

Next, for each sheet that has a major work assignment ask the question, "To accomplish this work assignment, what tasks must be performed or delivered?" Begin each task with an active verb since you are listing the action or performance that needs to be done. Figure 5-2 shows the breakdown of tasks for each of the major work assignments in our hypothetical project. (At this point in the work breakdown process, do not impose sequence into the work tasks.) Notice that there is only one task for each of the first two work assignments (assess requirements and design). Depending on the nature of the project, sometimes you may determine that the major work assignments sufficiently describe a process for developing a portion of the end product or end service (e.g., an in-house product development or systems development life cycle). We have used the first two work assignments to illustrate this occurrence.

Following are sample categories of major work assignments that can be used to construct a work breakdown structure:

## Sample Categories for Major Work Assignments

- *Components of the product:* internal, external, peripherals
- *Functions:* word processing, calculations, filing
- *Organizational units:* units, departments, branches
- *Geographical areas:* states, regions, cities
- *Cost accounts:* accounts assigned to parts of the project
- *Time phases:* initiation, design, development
- *Phases:* marketing, design, construction, training, financing

Break down the work efforts until you (or the person responsible for the area) can assign to them reliable *effort estimates* (the amount of effort time needed to accomplish the work task).

When you define the lowest level of detail, assign a person or functional area to take responsibility for doing the work and commit to a deliverable—the end product of the effort that comprises the work task. In other words, the work task (verb) results in a deliverable (noun). This deliverable can be measured and quality assured.

**Figure 5-1.** Work breakdown structure shell.

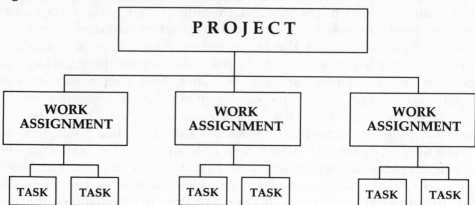

In order to determine if the WBS is complete and accurate, ask yourself the following questions:

- Is it broken down to the level of detail that guarantees control to the project manager?
- Do the work efforts at the lowest level begin with an active verb? (If they are phases, components of the product, or areas of responsibility, the WBS is not decomposed completely.)
- Does each activity result in a deliverable and have someone accountable for completing the activity on time, within budget, and of the quality acceptable?

If the answers to these questions are yes, the WBS is complete.

## Project Network

The WBS defines the tasks logically; then the network organizes them sequentially. Every work task in the WBS must also appear in the network. The network analyzes the sequence of task execution and portrays it in a diagram to ensure that the team is in agreement about the sequence. The team must feel that the sequence provides them with all prerequisites to their tasks. The objective of the network is to portray visually the relationships of work activities to each other. A network demonstrates these relationships and communicates them more clearly to project team members and to managers than any other technique.

There are two options for producing a network: (1) Draw the network free form (a right-brained, visual approach) or (2) determine the immediate predecessor(s) for each activity (left-brained, analytical approach) from which the network is generated.

**Figure 5-2.** Work breakdown structure tree chart for a sample project.

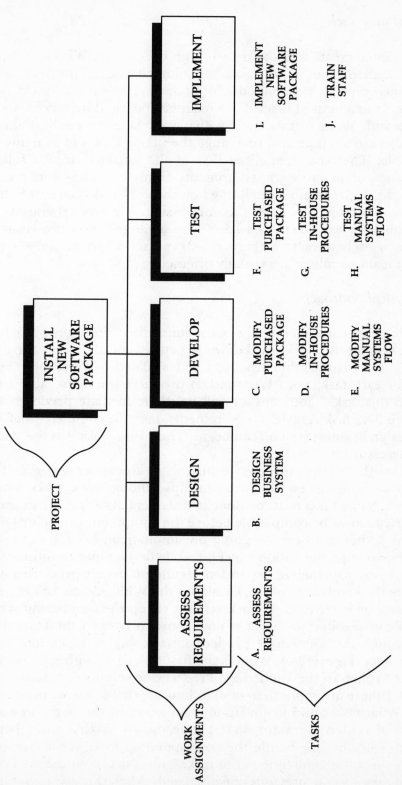

## Visual Approach

In order to create a visual network, go back to the WBS and separately label each of the work tasks. You may choose to produce labels on gummed slips (as we mentioned in Chapter 4, this is our favorite), 3 × 5 cards, or magnetized labels for a magnetic board. The specific tool is not important. What is important is that your labeling method allow team members to arrange and rearrange the network flow in as many ways as possible. The basic sequential flow of the network usually follows the sequence of major work assignments from the WBS—but not always, since the project team is analyzing how the work tasks can best fit together in a whole project, not just the work assignment areas themselves. Once the labels of work activities have been arranged, you can draw arrows between each work task (Figure 5-3), a useful way to show a network when team members are visually oriented.

## Analytical Approach

In this approach, define the most immediate predecessor(s) for each work task on the work breakdown structure, and then prepare a dependency analysis worksheet that can be translated to a network (Figure 5-4). For each task, ask, "What task(s) produces the deliverable I need to begin this task?" Your answer will be the immediate predecessor(s). In Figure 5-4, Task A, assess requirements, must be completed before Task B, design business system, can begin. Therefore, Task A is the immediate predecessor for Task B.

Another name for this technique is *dependency analysis*. The key purpose is to review the relationships among work tasks within the project. Some tasks must be done in a sequential order; for example, the electricity must be compatible before the equipment can be installed and tested. Other tasks can be going on simultaneously—for example, preparing an implementation checklist while development continues.

In order to analyze dependencies and ultimately produce a network, isolate the lowest level of work tasks on the WBS. Assign an identification number or letter to each work activity. (Keep the numbering scheme as simple as possible so that it is not a burden later in the project.) Then determine the immediate predecessor(s) using a dependency analysis worksheet (Figure 5-4). What is the first task that can begin this project? Put a hyphen in the Immediate Predecessor column beside this task (or tasks if there are more than one) to indicate that it has no predecessor.

What task could begin upon completion of the beginning activity? Write the identifiers for that predecessor—in this case, beginning task(s)—on the line beside the corresponding task. What task could be going on at the same time as this task? This task is now assigned the same predecessor as the previous one discussed. When there are no other tasks

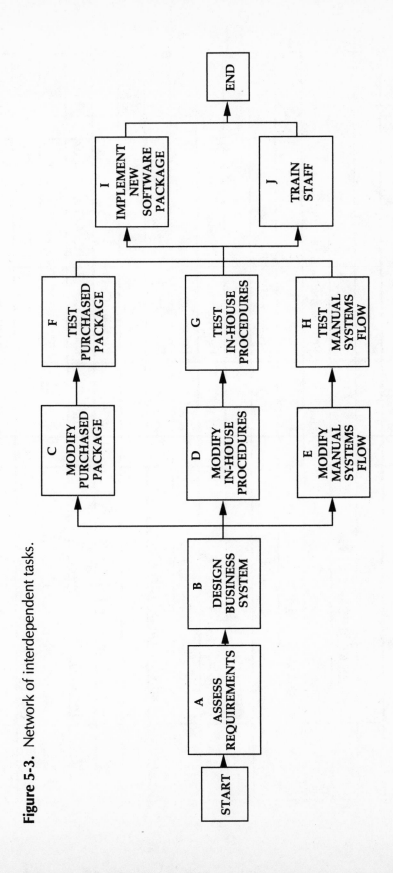

**Figure 5-3.** Network of interdependent tasks.

**Figure 5-4.** Task list with dependencies.

| TASK ID | TASK | TASK OWNER | DELIVERABLE(S) | IMMEDIATE PREDECESSOR |
|---|---|---|---|---|
| | **ASSESS REQUIREMENTS** | | | |
| A | Assess Requirements | Joan R. | Requirements Document | – |
| | **DESIGN** | | | |
| B | Design Business System | Bob S. | Project Definition | A |
| | **DEVELOP** | | | |
| C | Modify Purchased Package | Guy R. | Reprogrammed Package | B |
| D | Modify In-House Procedures | Marie S. | Procedures Manual | B |
| E | Modify Manual Systems Flow | Bob S. | Flowcharts | B |
| | **TEST** | | | |
| F | Test Purchased Package | Guy R. | Package Online | C |
| G | Test In-House Procedures | Marie S. | User Standards/Procedures In Place | D |
| H | Test Manual Systems Flow | Bob S. | Operational Procedures In Place | E |
| | **IMPLEMENT** | | | |
| I | Implement New Software Package | Joan R. | "Live" System | F,G,H |
| J | Train Staff | Marie S. | Trained Staff | F,G,H |

that could be going on at the same time, ask, "What task could be going on next?" Continue this process of chronologically walking through the project, but beware of redundancy. Use only the most immediate predecessor or predecessors.

Next, validate the dependency analysis worksheet. All task identifiers must appear in the Immediate Predecessor column unless the task is one of the last in the project. Look down the Immediate Predecessor column and determine if every work task identifier (in your WBS) appears. If it does not, ask, "Is this one of the final tasks of the project?" If the answer is yes, the WBS is validated. If the answer is no—that is, it isn't the last or one of the final tasks in the project—you have forgotten to make it a predecessor to something. Check your logic.

Now plot the work tasks onto the network. Draw a Start box on a blank sheet of paper in the vertical center toward the far left of the paper (the planning chart will branch to the right, top and bottom). At the Start box, burst all of the starting work tasks. In our example, we have only one starting task, Task A. Draw a dependency arrow from the Start box to each of the starting tasks (again, work tasks with no predecessor).

Build the chain by taking any task (or combination of tasks) now diagrammed on the network and searching for them in the immediate predecessor column. When you find them, expand the network accordingly. Let the immediate predecessor column drive the interpretation onto the network. You are developing a series of chains; each activity that appears on the network is merely a link in that chain. Once the link is attached to the chain, the Immediate Predecessor column tells which link or links must be attached next. Figure 5-3 shows how to use multiple dependency arrows when two or more activities burst out or converge; Tasks C, D, and E all share the same predecessor, Task B. Use the following guidelines when developing the network chart:

## Guidelines for Developing a Network Chart

- Don't worry about time estimates or drawing the network chart to scale. Concentrate on the relationships. The chart aesthetics can be improved later.
- Make sure there is only one Start box and one End box.
- Do not allow any task to dangle. Every task must connect to another task or to the start or end of the project. In other words, every task must be integrated into the framework of the network chart. If several tasks are all ending tasks, tie them together to one End box.
- Indicate key go/no-go points in this network chart.
- Remember that this is a communication tool; it must be clear to all who use it.

## Estimating Techniques

Estimating is not your best guess. It is not trying to reach a challenge. It is not succumbing to somebody else's demands. Here are a few more examples of what estimating is not: an estimate is not what we estimated the last time; not what we estimated the last time plus how much we slipped; not a conservative number with lots of padding; not taking someone else's estimate and then doubling it, and then increasing the units of time by one; not providing the expected or "right" answer.

Remember, the word *estimate* is defined in *Webster's Tenth New Collegiate Dictionary* as "an opinion or judgment of the nature, character, or quality of a . . . thing" or "a rough or approximate calculation." Many of us think of an estimate in these terms. However, the dictionary also defines an estimate as "a numerical value obtained from a statistical sample and assigned to a population parameter." That means that an estimate can and should be more than a guess, educated or otherwise. We will look at a technique that can make your estimates more credible (with exertion and effort, though).

Estimating in project management is a forecasting technique for determining the amount of effort time and elapsed time required to complete the work tasks of a project. We are attempting to forecast or predict how long the actual effort or work will take, how many human resources will be required, and the elapsed time or duration for completing the tasks.

Figure 5-5 shows a framework for developing a forecasting model. In order to determine the effort time and elapsed time required to complete a project task, we need to consider the key variables that affect it. (Effort time is defined as the amount of a person's actual effort given to the task. Elapsed time is the duration between when the task begins and ends.) For example, in the blank circles marked with directed forward effort, we could write the key variables that affect our estimates of the time to complete some of the work tasks in our sample project. Typical variables are the expertise or skill level necessary to perform the task(s); the job knowledge required before a team member can become productive; the number of people working on the task; or the number of tasks a single team member is working on simultaneously. In the blank circles directed forward effort, we could write the key variables that affect our estimates of the elapsed time necessary to complete some of these tasks. Typical variables are waiting for approvals, waiting for vendor shipments, and dead time.

## Critical Path Analysis

The *critical path* is the longest sequential series of tasks leading from the start to the end of the project. It is important to identify the critical path

**Figure 5-5.** Forecast method.

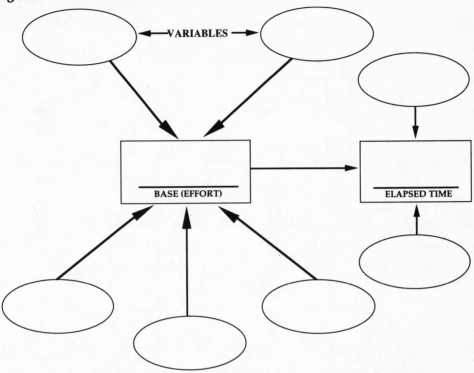

because a delay in any task on it could delay the entire project. Moreover, should someone request a shorter time frame, you could use a backward planning approach to the critical path and compress it, or during the project, you could manage by concentrating on critical path tasks.

In order to determine the critical path, post the elapsed time estimate for each work task to the network diagram. Figure 5-6 illustrates the network with an accompanying key. This key provides a useful and efficient way to calculate the critical path as well as various start and finish times. The elapsed time estimate for each task is written in the top left corner of the bottom quadrant (we will explain the remaining key indicators shortly). Add the elapsed time estimate for tasks along every path to determine the longest path. This path is the critical path and represents the estimated elapsed time of the project (symbolized by $T_E$). In the example (Figure 5-6), the critical path is A-B-E-H-I, and the total elapsed time for the project is 10.0 months. The noncritical paths in this network diagram include A-B-C-F-I (with an elapsed time of 8.5 months), A-B-D-G-I (with an elapsed time of 7.5 months), A-B-C-F-J (with an elapsed time of 7.5 months), A-B-D-G-J (with an elapsed time of 6.5 months), and A-B-E-H-J (with an elapsed time of 9.0 months). Keep in mind that tasks A, B, E, H, and I are also tasks on the critical path.

Now let's look at the other key indicators on the critical path.

**Figure 5-6.** Task sequence and critical path.

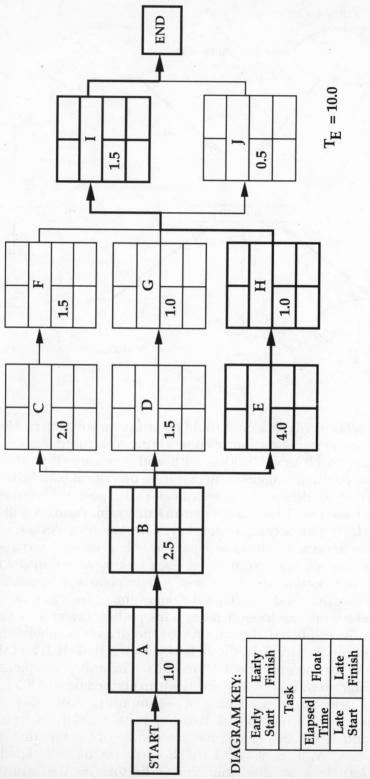

$T_E$ = Completion time: Time of the longest or critical path (in months)

DIAGRAM KEY:

| Early Start | Early Finish |
|---|---|
| Task | |
| Elapsed Time | Float |
| Late Start | Late Finish |

Suppose you want to determine the earliest start and finish dates for the critical path. How would you proceed? Look at the two boxes in the top row of the key on Figure 5-7. In the box on the left side, record the early start times for each task, and in the box on the right side, record the early finish times for each task. Early Start (ES) can be calculated by posting zero for the starting tasks (those with no predecessors) and using the early finish times of the previous task. Early Finish (EF) can be calculated by adding together the early start time for each task and the same task's elapsed time estimate.

Let's work through an example. Assume that the start is Day 0. This is the earliest you could start Task A. If Task A takes one month, then the earliest that Task A could be completed would be one month from the start of the project. In this case, Task B follows Task A. The earliest it can start is when the preceding Task A is completed at 1. Therefore, Task B has an early start of 1, and because Task B takes 2.5 units of time, the earliest Task B can be finished is 1 plus 2.5, which is 3.5. Keep in mind that the critical path's early finish always takes precedence over the other paths.

In order to calculate the late start and late finish dates for the critical path, refer to the two boxes in the bottom row of the key in Figure 5-7. The latest date on which each task can finish (LF) is the late start of the succeeding task. The latest date on which each task can start (LS) is the late finish of the preceding task minus the elapsed time. For example, the sample project ends at Month 10, so the late finish for each of the final tasks, I and J, in our example is 10 (Figure 5-7). The latest that each task could be started is the late finish of the task minus its elapsed time. For example, Task I has a late finish of 10 and a late start of 8.5, which was derived by subtracting its elapsed time, 1.5, from the late finish, 10. Moving backward on the path, the late finish of Task F is the late start of Task I, or 8.5.

There is one more important calculation to make regarding the sequence of tasks surrounding the critical path: float. *Float* is the leeway time existing within noncritical path tasks. Technically, float is the difference between the late finish and early finish times for tasks on noncritical paths. In Figure 5-7, the float calculations for each task are recorded in the top right-hand corner of the bottom quadrant. For Task J, the float is 1.0 month (late finish of 10.0 months minus early finish of 9 months). Keep in mind that float occurs only on noncritical paths. Did you notice that the ES, EF and LS, LF are the same for tasks on the critical path? Also, two or more tasks on the same noncritical path will calculate the same float, which they must share. So the float time of 1.5 months for Tasks C and F must be shared between them, and the float time of 2.5 months for Tasks D and G must be shared.

**Figure 5-7.** Development of early start, early finish, late start, and late finish.

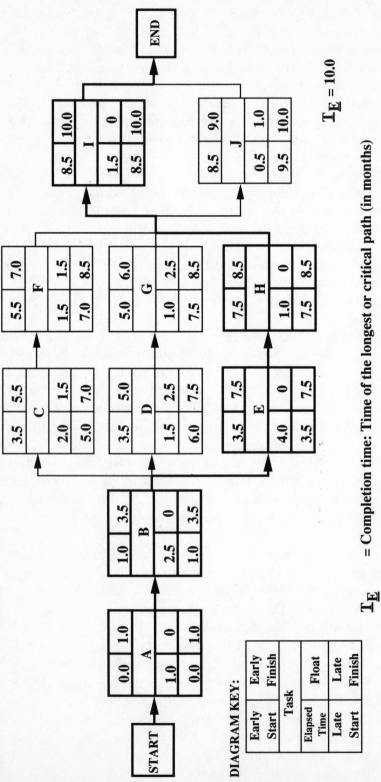

DIAGRAM KEY:

| Early Start | Early Finish |
|---|---|
| Task | |
| Elapsed Time | Float |
| Late Start | Late Finish |

$T_E$ = Completion time: Time of the longest or critical path (in months)

## Scheduling

The major objective of a schedule, sometimes referred to as a Gantt chart, is to place the data from the previous four techniques—the WBS, the network, the estimates, and the critical path analysis—on a time scale. In order to develop a comprehensive time scale, it is important that we see when work tasks start and end, which are critical path tasks, which tasks have float and where it has been allocated, and what the dependencies of tasks are to one another.

In order to plot the schedule, use a calendar format similar to the one shown in Figure 5-8. The units of time are recorded along the horizontal axis and the task identifications are recorded along the vertical axis. In our example, we have ten months of time and ten work tasks (A–J). Beginning with the critical path, plot Task A on the schedule with an up-triangle indicating the early start (zero in this case) and a horizontal line drawn to a down-triangle indicating the early finish (one month). Continue plotting the tasks on the critical path (B, E, and H), being sure to connect each work task vertically with its immediate predecessor(s). When you come to the first critical path work task that has input from a noncritical path(s) (Task I in our example), plot the parallel noncritical paths (C, F and D, G) before plotting this next task. Use slash lines to depict the float at the end of the noncritical path(s), unless you have determined another special allocation. In our example, the float for Tasks C and F (1.5 months) begins at the end of Task F (Month 7) and continues to Month 8.5. Similarly, the float for Tasks D and G (2.5 months) begins at the end of Task G (Month 6) and continues to Month 8.5. Work in this fashion until all activities have been translated to the schedule. In this way, we have planned to complete the tasks (except Task J) as soon as possible and to use the float at the end of our project. We have decided to put Task J on its late schedule since training is best done just before people need to use the skills. As a result, Task J is now added to the critical path.

Initially, during planning, the float can be used as a buffer to manipulate the schedule to be more compatible with resource availability. Later, during monitoring and controlling, float tells you when a particular task may be in jeopardy. If a task has no float, it is on the critical path. If a task has slipped, using up all of its float, it is behind schedule, and you must find a way to recoup that time on the critical path. If the task has float and it is behind schedule, watch that task carefully. If the task has used all its float time and is stretching beyond that, recognize that it has become a critical task, with a changed critical path, and will affect the completion of the total project. Not only must you ensure that this activity is completed as quickly as possible, but those responsible for succeeding activities dependent on that late task must be informed. The

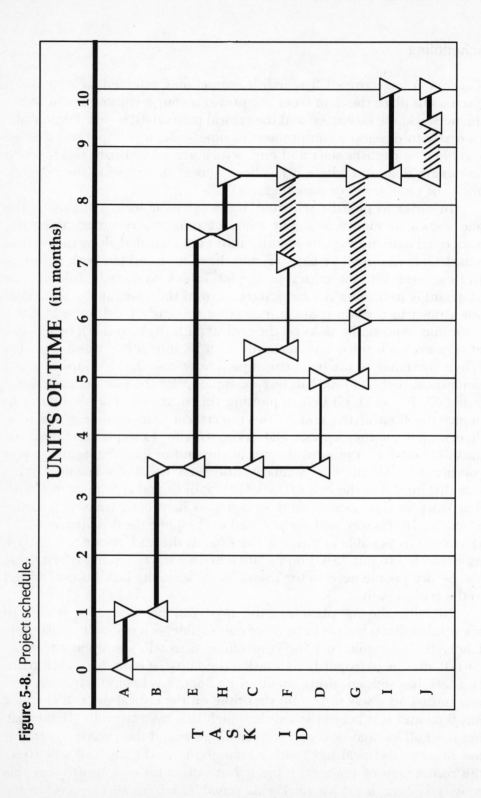

**Figure 5-8.** Project schedule.

lost time must be made up in one of the succeeding activities to complete the project on time.

## Resource Loading

*Resource loading* is used to determine how resources will be allocated over the duration of a project and how to verify that they are being allocated correctly. In other words, the purpose is to ensure that no team members are ever overloaded. There are several options to determine resource loading:

1. Verify by name of employee that the number of activities (or projects) any one person (or pool) is working on simultaneously is reasonable. For example, according to the diagram shown in Figure 5-9, Marie Scotto (MS) appears to be very busy during the middle of the project.

2. Sum the percentage of time each team member plans to commit to each activity (or project) in a single time frame in order to determine a total percentage greater than or less than the time the individual has available. The diagram shown in Figure 5-10, for example, indicates that MS has scheduled 150 percent of her time between Months 9.5 and 10 (summing vertically during this time period would give us 50 percent of her time on Task I and 100 percent of her time on Task J).

3. Calculate the individual effort allocation for each team member. The diagram shown in Figure 5-11 points out that Marie's time will be spent working on Tasks A, B, D, E, G, I, and J. The individual effort estimate for her time on each of these tasks is posted vertically in the boxes falling under her name. For example, her individual effort estimate for Task A is .1. This means that Marie will be spending .1 effort months on this task. The total effort estimate of 1.0 for all team members is located in the top box under the column heading Total Effort Estimate.

For the example, we have chosen to use 1.0 as a standard figure to represent forty hours of work, or one week. This estimated forty hours of total effort for Task A is determined by summing the individual effort estimates of the team members who will be working on this task—in this case, Joan's .5 (twenty hours) and the .1 estimate for the remaining team members (Bob, Guy, Marie, Jean, and Seth). If we take this individual effort estimate for each team member on each task and divide it by the elapsed time for the task, we will have calculated individual effort allocation. We will have dispersed the estimate of each team member's effort time over the elapsed time of the task. As a result, we now have a precise measure for determining how team members' times will be used for each task when posted onto the time schedule.

*(Text continues on page 77.)*

**Figure 5-9.** Resource assignment posted on schedule.

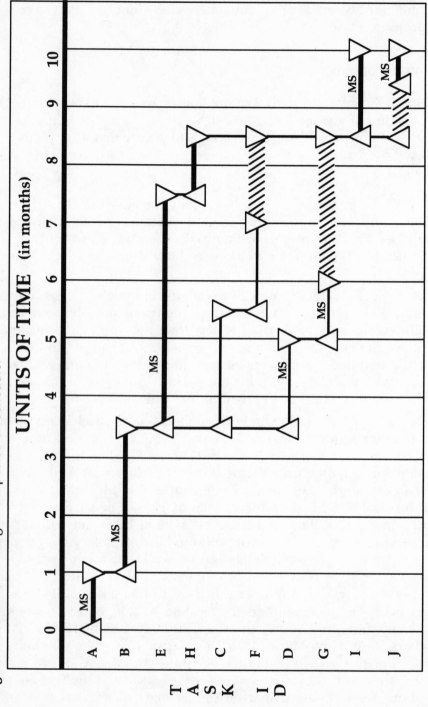

**Figure 5-10.** Percentage committed posted on schedule, for Marie S.

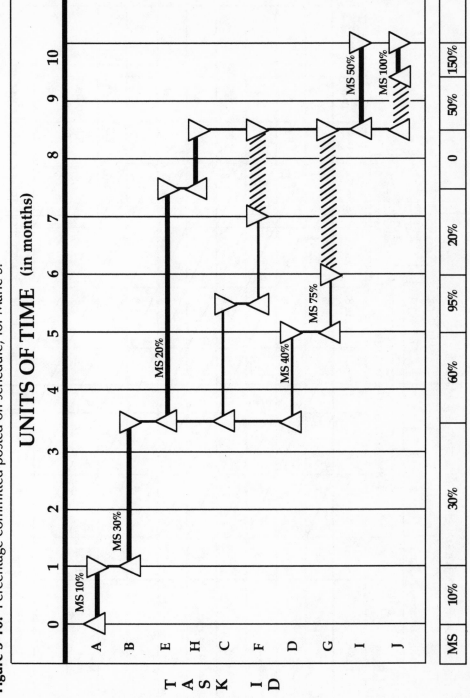

# Figure 5-11. Calculation of individual effort allocation for Marie S.

| PROJECT NAME | Install Purchased Package | PREPARED BY | J. Ryan | PAGE 1 | OF 1 |
|---|---|---|---|---|---|

PROJECT MANAGER J. Ryan

RESPONSIBILITY MATRIX

LEGEND: Prime or Support / Individual Effort Estimate

| TASK ID | TASK | IMMED PRED | Joan R. | Bob S. | Guy R. | Marie S. | Jean M. | Seth K. | TOTAL EFFORT (EST) | ELAPSED TIME | INDIVIDUAL EFFORT ALLOCATION |
|---|---|---|---|---|---|---|---|---|---|---|---|
| A | Assess Requirements | — | P .5 | S .1 | S .1 | S .1 | S .1 | S .1 | 1.0 | 1.0 | |
| B | Design Business System | A | S .75 | P 1.5 | S .75 | S .75 | | S 1.25 | 5.0 | 2.5 | |
| C | Modify Purchased Package | B | | | P 2.0 | | S 2.0 | | 4.0 | 2.0 | |
| D | Modify In-House Procedures | B | S .25 | S .5 | | P 1.0 | | S .5 | 2.25 | 1.5 | |
| E | Modify Manual Systems Flow | B | | P 1.0 | | S .7 | S .3 | | 2.0 | 4.0 | |
| F | Test Purchased Package | C | S .25 | | P 1.0 | | S .75 | S .25 | 2.25 | 1.5 | |
| G | Test In-House Procedures | D | S 1.0 | | | P 1.0 | | S 1.0 | 3.0 | 1.0 | |
| H | Test Manual Systems Flow | E | S .5 | P 1.0 | | | | S 1.0 | 2.5 | 1.0 | |
| I | Implement New Software Package | F,G,H | P .5 | S .5 | S .5 | S .5 | S .5 | S .5 | 3.0 | 1.5 | |
| J | Train Staff | F,G,H | | | | P .5 | | | .5 | .5 | |

Individual effort estimate ÷ Elapsed time = Individual effort allocation

Let's go back to Marie. The last column in the diagram Figure 5-12 shows Marie's individual effort allocation for the tasks she will be working on. Next let's post these allocations to the schedule. You try. In Figure 5-13, each team member's individual effort allocations are posted above their corresponding task in the diagram. Post Marie's allocations above the tasks on which she will be working. Then for each of the major time periods blocked out in the grid below the time schedule, write down Marie's total individual effort allocation. When you have completed these two steps, compare your answers with those shown in Figure 5-14.

As you can see, Marie will be working a total of .10 (or 10 percent of her time) during Month 1; .30 during Months 1–3.5; .85 from Months 3.5–5; 1.18 during both time periods in Month 5; .18 from Month 6 to 7.5; 0 from 7.5–8.5; .33 from 8.5–9.5; and 1.33 during the last half-month of the project. The histogram in Figure 5-15 provides a picture of how Marie's individual effort allocation is used over the life cycle of the project. (A histogram is a graphic representation of how work effort changes over time during the project.) We have graphed Marie's effort allocation according to the vertical axis, designated FTE (full time equivalency). In other words, 1.00 FTE is equal to forty hours of work. Anything above this marker is considered overtime; anything below might be considered underutilization. Marie obviously is working overtime during Month 5 and the last half of Month 9.

Figures 5-16, 5-17, and 5-18 present the same resource analysis for the total effort allocation of the project team. Later in the chapter, we will consider how to balance or level individual and team allocations.

## Key Business Applications

Two business decisions often need to be made when applying planning techniques: making adjustments to the schedule in order to meet mandated target dates and leveling or smoothing out overloaded resources.

### *Meeting Mandated Target Dates*

Imagine that you and your team have produced a schedule. But then—for some legitimate or whimsical reason—the client or senior management requires that the project be completed more quickly. What do you do now?

The original duration of the project was determined by isolating the longest series (or path) of activities—the critical path. Therefore, it is the critical path activities that must be shortened. This is commonly called **critical path compression.** By compressing some activities on the critical path, you can shorten the duration of the project. The major technique

**Figure 5-12.** Calculation of effort allocation for Marie S.

| PROJECT NAME | Install Purchased Package | | PREPARED BY | J. Ryan | | PAGE 1 | OF 1 |
|---|---|---|---|---|---|---|---|

PROJECT MANAGER J. Ryan

LEGEND:
Prime or Support

Individual Effort Estimate

RESPONSIBILITY MATRIX

| TASK ID | TASK | IMMED PRED | Joan R. | Bob S. | Guy R. | Marie S. | Jean M. | Seth K. | TOTAL EFFORT (EST) | ELAPSED TIME | INDIVIDUAL EFFORT ALLOCATION |
|---|---|---|---|---|---|---|---|---|---|---|---|
| A | Assess Requirements | – | P / .5 | S / .1 | S / .1 | S / .1 | S / .1 | S / .1 | 1.0 | 1.0 | .1 |
| B | Design Business System | A | S / .75 | P / 1.5 | S / .75 | S / .75 | | S / 1.25 | 5.0 | 2.5 | .3 |
| C | Modify Purchased Package | B | | | P / 2.0 | | S / 2.0 | | 4.0 | 2.0 | |
| D | Modify In-House Procedures | B | S / .25 | S / .5 | | P / 1.0 | S / | S / .5 | 2.25 | 1.5 | .67 |
| E | Modify Manual Systems Flow | B | | P / 1.0 | | S / .7 | S / .3 | | 2.0 | 4.0 | .18 |
| F | Test Purchased Package | C | S / .25 | | P / 1.0 | | S / .75 | S / .25 | 2.25 | 1.5 | |
| G | Test In-House Procedures | D | S / 1.0 | | | P / 1.0 | | S / 1.0 | 3.0 | 1.0 | 1.0 |
| H | Test Manual Systems Flow | E | S / .5 | P / 1.0 | | S / | | S / 1.0 | 2.5 | 1.0 | |
| I | Implement New Software Package | F,G,H | P / .5 | S / .5 | S / .5 | S / .5 | S / .5 | S / .5 | 3.0 | 1.5 | .33 |
| J | Train Staff | F,G,H | | | | P / .5 | | | .5 | .5 | 1.0 |

Individual effort estimate ÷ Elapsed time = Individual effort allocation

**Figure 5-13.** Calculation of effort allocation for Marie S.

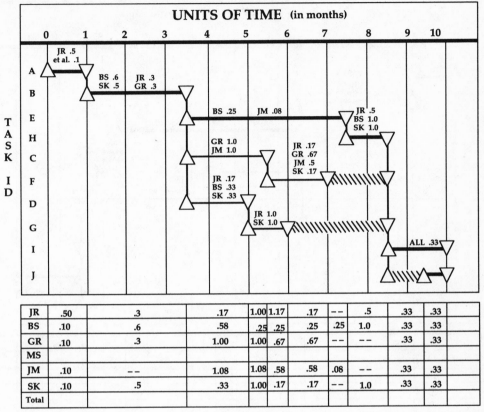

| | 0–1 | 1–2 | 2–3 | 3–4 | 4–5 | 5–6 | 6–7 | 7–8 | 8–9 | 9–10 |
|---|---|---|---|---|---|---|---|---|---|---|
| JR | .50 | .3 | | .17 | 1.00 | 1.17 | .17 | -- | .5 | .33 | .33 |
| BS | .10 | .6 | | .58 | .25 | .25 | .25 | .25 | 1.0 | .33 | .33 |
| GR | .10 | .3 | | 1.00 | 1.00 | .67 | .67 | -- | -- | .33 | .33 |
| MS | | | | | | | | | | | |
| JM | .10 | -- | | 1.08 | 1.08 | .58 | .58 | .08 | -- | .33 | .33 |
| SK | .10 | .5 | | .33 | 1.00 | .17 | .17 | -- | 1.0 | .33 | .33 |
| Total | | | | | | | | | | | |

of critical path compression is to break a critical path activity into overlapping tasks, a technique sometimes called **fast tracking the project.** There are five alternatives for fast tracking:

1. *Decompose the work even further.* Break the critical path activity into subtasks, which are scheduled, to the greatest extent possible, in parallel. The more subtasks that can be scheduled in parallel, the faster the activity can be completed.

2. *Alter the finish-to-start relationships.* The relationships we have discussed so far have been finish-to-start relationships; that is, one task cannot start until its predecessor task has been completely finished. There are two types of finish-to-start precedence relationships: mandatory and judgmental. A mandatory finish-to-start relationship cannot be changed without violating a law, regulation, or corporate policy; therefore, it cannot be altered through negotiation. Even if the project schedule is unacceptable to the client, mandatory finish-to-start relationships must be preserved. In our experience, though, fewer than half of all finish-to-start relationships are mandatory. (The percentage tends to

**Figure 5-14.** Calculation of effort allocation for Marie S.

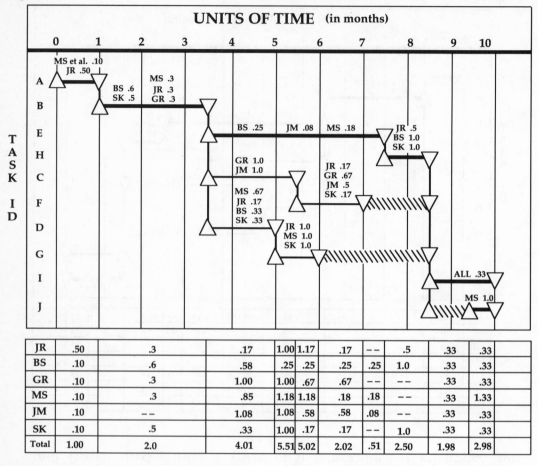

| | | | | | | | | | | |
|---|---|---|---|---|---|---|---|---|---|---|
| JR | .50 | .3 | .17 | 1.00 | 1.17 | .17 | -- | .5 | .33 | .33 |
| BS | .10 | .6 | .58 | .25 | .25 | .25 | .25 | 1.0 | .33 | .33 |
| GR | .10 | .3 | 1.00 | 1.00 | .67 | .67 | -- | -- | .33 | .33 |
| MS | .10 | .3 | .85 | 1.18 | 1.18 | .18 | .18 | -- | .33 | 1.33 |
| JM | .10 | -- | 1.08 | 1.08 | .58 | .58 | .08 | -- | .33 | .33 |
| SK | .10 | .5 | .33 | 1.00 | .17 | .17 | -- | 1.0 | .33 | .33 |
| Total | 1.00 | 2.0 | 4.01 | 5.51 | 5.02 | 2.02 | .51 | 2.50 | 1.98 | 2.98 |

vary from industry to industry; safety-related nuclear industry projects have a higher percentage of mandatory relationships than almost any other industry.)

A judgmental finish-to-start relationship is one in which the task owner of the successor task sees a risk in overlapping the tasks. The finish-to-start relationship is a result of the team member's believing that it is not prudent to overlap the two tasks in question. This is a statement of professional judgment on the part of the person responsible for the successor task. All other things being equal, it is wise for you to respect this judgment of the task leader and to leave the finish-to-start relationship alone. However, when altering one or more of the judgmental finish-to-start relationships makes the difference between undertaking or shelving the project, it may be appropriate to negotiate revisions to these judgmental relationships.

You and the task owner must remember that altering the judgmental finish-to-start relationship represents an additional risk, which depends

*(Text continues on page 85.)*

**Figure 5-15.** Individual resource loading histogram for Marie S.

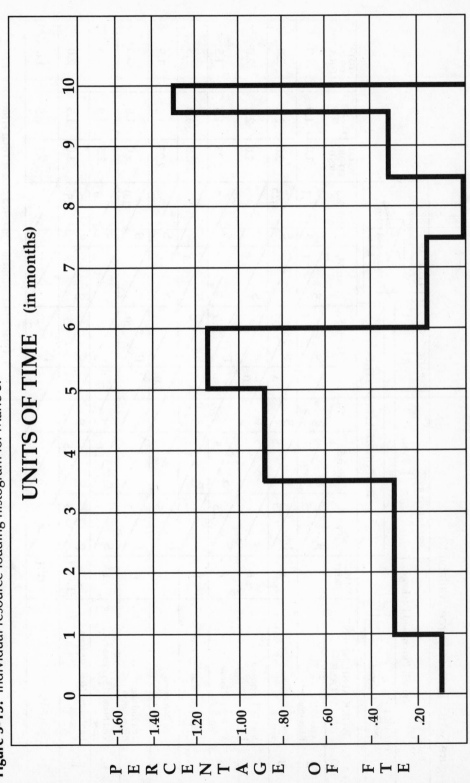

**Figure 5-16.** Team resource availability.

PROJECT NAME: Install Purchased Package  
PREPARED BY: J. Ryan  
PAGE 1 OF 1  
PROJECT MANAGER: J. Ryan  

RESPONSIBILITY MATRIX

LEGEND:  
Prime or Support / Individual Effort Estimate

| TASK ID | WORK ASSIGNMENT – TASK – | IMMED PRED | Joan R. | Bob S. | Guy R. | Marie S. | Jean M. | Seth K. | TOTAL EFFORT (EST) | ELAPSED TIME | TOTAL EFFORT ALLOCATION |
|---|---|---|---|---|---|---|---|---|---|---|---|
| A | Assess Requirements | – | P .5 | S .1 | S .1 | S .1 | S .1 | S .1 | 1.0 | 1.0 | 1.0 |
| B | Design Business System | A | S .75 | P 1.5 | S .75 | S .75 | | S 1.25 | 5.0 | 2.5 | 2.0 |
| C | Modify Purchased Package | B | | | P 2.0 | | S 2.0 | | 4.0 | 2.0 | 2.0 |
| D | Modify In-House Procedures | B | S .25 | S .5 | | P 1.0 | | S .5 | 2.25 | 1.5 | 1.5 |
| E | Modify Manual Systems Flow | B | | P 1.0 | | S .7 | S .3 | | 2.0 | 4.0 | .5 |
| F | Test Purchased Package | C | S .25 | | P 1.0 | | S .75 | S .25 | 2.25 | 1.5 | 1.5 |
| G | Test In-House Procedures | D | S 1.0 | | | P 1.0 | | S 1.0 | 3.0 | 1.0 | 3.0 |
| H | Test Manual Systems Flow | E | S .5 | P 1.0 | | | | S 1.0 | 2.5 | 1.0 | 2.5 |
| I | Implement New Software Package | F,G,H | P .5 | S .5 | S .5 | S .5 | S .5 | S .5 | 3.0 | 1.5 | 2.0 |
| J | Train Staff | F,G,H | | | | P .5 | | | .5 | .5 | 1.0 |

Total effort estimate ÷ Elapsed time = Total effort allocation

**Figure 5-17.** Team resource availability and scheduling.

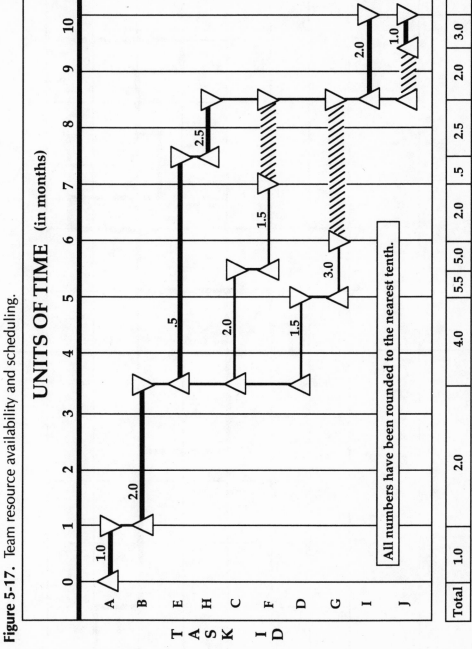

UNITS OF TIME (in months)

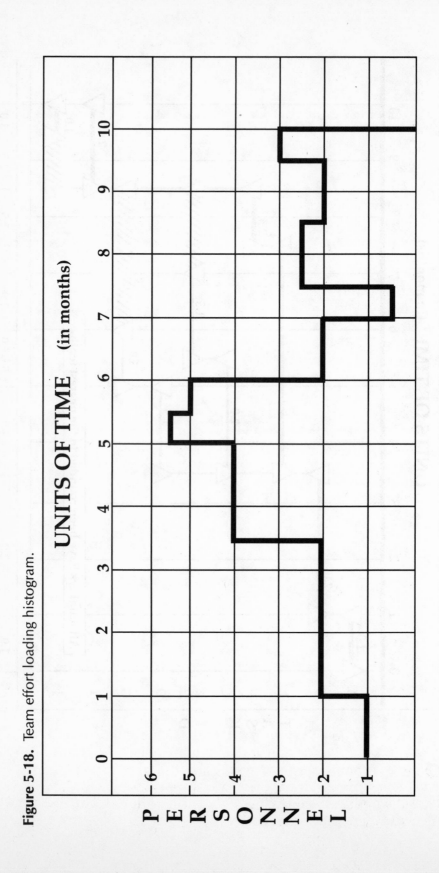

**Figure 5-18.** Team effort loading histogram.

on the specifics of the tasks being overlapped. There is always a risk when such action is taken; although the period of performance for the project may be shortened and the cost may not increase, the decision has some potential to backfire, causing both a schedule delay and increased costs.

Relationships that are judgmental can be reevaluated as partial relationships. There are several approaches:

1. Establish percentage dependencies in which the critical path activity requires less than 100 percent of its immediate predecessor. For example, perhaps only 20 percent of the entire design process needs to be finished before development can be started.
2. Try start-to-start relationships with a lag. The critical path activity starts at the same time as its predecessor, with a predetermined lag or delay time. For example, development can start one month after design has started.
3. Choose a finish-to-finish relationship with a lead. The critical path activity must be completed at a specified number of time units before its successor is completed. For example, the design work must be completed two weeks before the development is scheduled to be completed.
4. Reevaluate and break dependencies since dependencies indicate that one activity must be completed before another can begin. For example, the design of the product is not going to begin until funding is obtained. But what if there is a marketing window to be met? It may be wise to break the conservative relationship of receiving funding before the start of design, starting the design at the same time that the acquisition of funding begins. This option may put the project at a higher risk, but if the higher risk is agreed to, the alternative is viable.

Implementation of any of these alternatives assumes that there are enough resources available to work on all of the subtasks that would be going on in parallel.

3. *Assign more resources.* There are several ways to assign more resources to the critical work activities. First, try to work within the resources already assigned to the project. Perhaps a project member is not working on the critical path and could give the project more time.

You could analyze the noncritical paths to determine if any resource with the correct skill mix is available to be reassigned to other, parallel critical path activities, thus shortening the duration of the critical path activities. Remember that removing a resource from a non–critical path activity will lengthen the duration of that activity and that the noncritical path may turn into the critical path.

If there are an inadequate number of people assigned to the project, recruit from within the organization or from outside contractors. Continually reevaluate the extra dollars that these resources will cost the project. Keep in mind, however, that the resources must have the appropriate skills required by the critical path activities. Do not assign resources to an activity based upon their time availability alone.

4. *Remove an activity from the critical path.* This option certainly will shorten the critical path, but it may also reduce the functionality of the end product or increase the risk of failure on the project.

5. *Expedite a critical path activity.* The duration of a critical path activity may be shortened by making it more efficient or finding a faster way to get the job done. This may mean spending more money. However, the additional cost may have a positive return on investment by getting the project done sooner, with the benefits accruing at an earlier date. *This does not mean slicing days off the estimate with no thought of the reality of the new estimate.*

Too often when the project planner is given a mandated completion date shorter than the derived critical path time estimates, additional dollars and/or resources are requested as a knee-jerk reaction. Through the use of some of these techniques, responding to a constrained time frame may be accomplished without spending additional resources or dollars.

### Resource Leveling

#### Leveling Within the Project

If there are resources that have been overloaded after they have been allocated, how do you level (or smooth) them out?

When supply falls short of demand, there are a number of approaches to leveling:

- Tasks can be shifted or extended within their float. This may eliminate unacceptable peaks without altering the cost of any part of the workload.
- Use overtime to meet the demand during the period of forecasted overutilization.
- Ask the team members to exert extra effort. Compensation or time off can be offered to staff members working a number of hours substantially in excess of the norm.
- Augment the resource pool through the use of temporary help. (This is often not feasible, however, due to the need to provide work space, tools, and facilities to the temporary workers.)

- Contract out a portion of the workload. This relieves the organization of the burden of providing space, tools, and facilities, but it also potentially increases the cost of achieving the organization's objectives.
- Increase the size of the resource pool permanently. If the forecast of supply versus demand yields multiple periods of overutilization well into the future, adding staff to the resource pool may be the most effective approach to manage the workload.
- Select a portion of the workload to be delayed beyond its approved completion date in order to eliminate the peaks in the demand for the resource. Performing this alternative, referred to as resource-constrained scheduling, requires an understanding of the relative priorities of each component of the project and nonproject workload of the resource pool.

When supply exceeds demand, some of these same approaches can be used to level demand:

- Tasks can be moved within their float to take advantage of the resource pool's available time.
- Overtime can be eliminated, and any temporary help being employed by the organization can be replaced with permanent staff.
- Management can consider reducing the size of the resource pool selectively if the forecast shows a prolonged period of oversupply.
- Low-priority work can be moved up in the organization's schedule to take advantage of the availability of the resources.

There are two other possibilities that represent unique opportunities during oversupply:

- Use these periods to develop new methods for the cost-effective performance of the work of the resource pool.
- Cross-train staff during these periods so that they can be allocated in the future to components of the workload they are not now qualified to perform.

### Leveling by the Functional Manager

Resource leveling on the part of the functional manager is a key element in efficient and cost-effective management of the organization's project workload. In order to perform resource leveling well, the functional managers must understand the objectives of the organization, be familiar with the relative priority of each component of the workload, and obtain the cooperation of project managers.

Problems of oversupply of resources and assets (underutilization) or excess demand for resources and assets (overutilization) are solved in the same manner. The following approaches, all of which require negotiation between the functional and the project managers, are helpful:

### Solving Resource Utilization Problems

> - Move tasks on any project, within float, to level demand.
> - Alter the time-cost-resource mix to level the demand. (This may alter the cost of the task.)
> - Use overtime to accommodate demand. (This may alter the cost of the task.)
> - Use temporary help, under the supervision of the functional unit, to address demand peaks. (This may alter the cost of the task.)
> - Rent equipment to address peak demands. (This may alter the cost of the task.)
> - Contract out a portion of the workload to address peak demands. (This may alter the cost of the task.)
> - Seek management permission to acquire additional resources or assets to address peak demands.

If the functional manager cannot resolve the problem with these techniques, the final alternative is to identify the lowest-priority project that is contributing to the unacceptable peak demand and delay it. This may require the approval of management and several group business managers, since it will alter an approved completion date. Plan revisions that must be made to resolve resource and asset demand problems must be forwarded to the project managers, so that they can produce updated plans. This step cannot be completed unless senior management establishes priorities for project and nonproject workloads. Senior management tends to make such priority decisions as they are required and to communicate them effectively. It is counterproductive to level demand for resources over a long time frame. The only constant in project management is change, and it is expected that demand for resources in future periods will change.

### *Project Budget*

The purpose of a project budget is to take each category of one-time developmental expenses (budgeted) and allocate it across the duration of the project, indicating when the dollars are committed or booked to be spent. This step has two parts:

1. *Allocate budget onto a cost spread sheet.* Based on the resource loading, the resource (labor) dollars required may be determined over time. Other categories of expenses may be spread across time and summed to determine a complete budget. Figure 5-19 shows a periodic cost spread sheet in which the budget is spread out on a month-to-month basis over the nine-month cycle of the project. Figure 5-20 shows a cumulative cost spread sheet in which the budget is spread out to date by period. Remember that the cost spread sheet is cumulative period to date. Validate the cost spread sheet, remembering that expenses can never decrease.
2. Plot the budget expenditures on a cost line graph in order to translate the cost spread sheet into a graphic representation. Draw the grid with "Units of Time" along the top and "Costs" along the left side of the grid, and plot the committed expenses in a line graph format (Figure 5-21). Create an individual line graph for each category of expenses as well. Validate the cost line graph by checking that it looks like an elongated capital letter S, or a straight diagonal, which is possible, but unlikely.

### Risk Assessment and Contingency Planning

Risk is a certainty in project planning; managing it can be the pivotal factor in successful project management. A sound approach to the management of risk requires an additional effort in planning but can achieve a worthwhile return on investment. **Risk analysis** is a what-if exercise to identify areas of concern. **Contingency planning** may mean making backup plans or more conservative scheduling of tasks and resources.

One way to introduce the subject of risk assessment is to ask the project team members to describe the unexpected things that have gone wrong during other projects on which they have worked. Perhaps management introduced new priorities; the best people suddenly were not available; the budget was reduced; another group or vendor was late; another group or vendor was over budget; another group or vendor made something that didn't work; or unforeseen technical problems appeared.

Isolate risk in the areas of the schedule (to include factors that may cause delays), resources (to include factors that may threaten availability), finances (to include factors that may threaten the project budget), and scope (to include factors that make the completion of the end product uncertain).

*(Text continues on page 93.)*

**Figure 5-19.** Periodic cost spread sheet.

TOTAL BUDGET $250K

P = Plan
A = Actual

## COSTS BY PERIOD (in months)

| COST CATEGORIES | 1 P | 1 A | 2 P | 2 A | 3 P | 3 A | 4 P | 4 A | 5 P | 5 A | 6 P | 6 A | 7 P | 7 A | 8 P | 8 A | 9 P | 9 A | 10 P | 10 A |
|---|---|---|---|---|---|---|---|---|---|---|---|---|---|---|---|---|---|---|---|---|
| EQUIPMENT | 0 | | 0 | | 10K | | 20K | | 20K | | 20K | | 2K | | 2K | | 0 | | | |
| SUPPLIES | 10K | | 2K | | 3K | | 5K | | 15K | | 5K | | 5K | | 5K | | 0 | | | |
| LABOR | 8K | | 12K | | 4K | | 12K | | 12K | | 30K | | 30K | | 12K | | 6K | | | |
| | | | | | | | | | | | | | | | | | | | | |
| | | | | | | | | | | | | | | | | | | | | |
| | | | | | | | | | | | | | | | | | | | | |
| | | | | | | | | | | | | | | | | | | | | |
| | | | | | | | | | | | | | | | | | | | | |
| | | | | | | | | | | | | | | | | | | | | |
| PERIOD TOTAL | 18K | | 14K | | 17K | | 37K | | 47K | | 55K | | 37K | | 19K | | 6K | | | |
| CUMULATIVE TOTAL | 18K | | 32K | | 49K | | 86K | | 133K | | 188K | | 225K | | 244K | | 250K | | | |

**Figure 5-20.** Cumulative cost spread sheet.

TOTAL BUDGET $250K

P = Plan
A = Actual

| COST CATEGORIES | PERIOD TO DATE BY PERIOD (in months) | | | | | | | | | | | | | | | | | | | |
|---|---|---|---|---|---|---|---|---|---|---|---|---|---|---|---|---|---|---|---|---|
| | 1 | | 2 | | 3 | | 4 | | 5 | | 6 | | 7 | | 8 | | 9 | | 10 | |
| | P | A | P | A | P | A | P | A | P | A | P | A | P | A | P | A | P | A | P | A |
| EQUIPMENT | 0 | | 0 | | 10K | | 30K | | 50K | | 70K | | 72K | | 74K | | 74K | | | |
| SUPPLIES | 10K | | 12K | | 15K | | 20K | | 35K | | 40K | | 45K | | 50K | | 50K | | | |
| LABOR | 8K | | 20K | | 24K | | 36K | | 48K | | 78K | | 108K | | 120K | | 126K | | | |
| | | | | | | | | | | | | | | | | | | | | |
| | | | | | | | | | | | | | | | | | | | | |
| | | | | | | | | | | | | | | | | | | | | |
| | | | | | | | | | | | | | | | | | | | | |
| | | | | | | | | | | | | | | | | | | | | |
| TOTAL | 18K | | 32K | | 49K | | 86K | | 133K | | 188K | | 225K | | 244K | | 250K | | | |

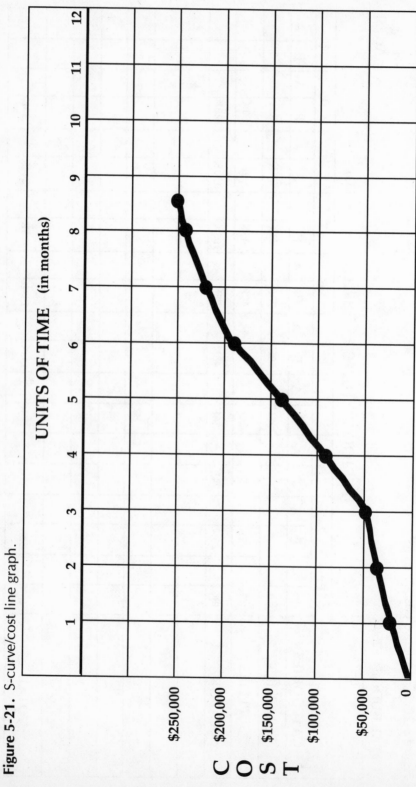

**Figure 5-21.** S-curve/cost line graph.

**Specific Risk Factors**

Schedule

- Tasks on the critical path
- Tasks that have several predecessors
- Tasks that have minimal float
- Optimistically estimated tasks
- Tasks reliant on external dependencies, such as vendor shipments
- Major milestones

Resources

- Tasks with one individual working alone
- Tasks with many people assigned
- Tasks using scarce resources
- Underskilled or unqualified people
- Illness and turnover

Budget

- Uncertainty of funds
- Shifts in budget priorities
- Uncertain resource costs

Scope

- Uncertainty of new product development
- Dynamics of customer requirements
- Availability of tools and/or techniques
- Large number of defects

Follow these key guidelines for developing contingency plans:

**Guidelines for Contingency Planning**

Revise the schedule by:

- Negotiating deadlines of high-risk tasks to accommodate potential slippage
- Scheduling tasks that can be postponed or canceled if necessary later in the project
- Conservatively estimating durations of tasks on the critical path
- Generating a schedule that takes the contingency into account

**Figure 5-22.** Contingency planning worksheet.

**High Risk Situation:** *

**Probable Cause(s):** **

| PROBABILITY |
|---|
| Hi=3;  Med=2;  Lo=1 |
| Score = |

| IMPACT |
|---|
| Hi=6;  Med=4;  Lo=2 |
| Score = |

|  | High Probability High Impact (Prepare Contingency Plan) | Low Probability High Impact (Prepare Contingency Plan) |
|---|---|---|
| 3 | High Probability Low Impact (Dealer's Choice) | |
| 2 | | Low Probability Low Impact (Forget it) |
| 1 | | |

P R O B A B I L I T Y

0    1    2    3    4    5    6

IMPACT

**Preventive Plan(s)****

**Contingency Plan(s)***

**Trigger Point(s)**

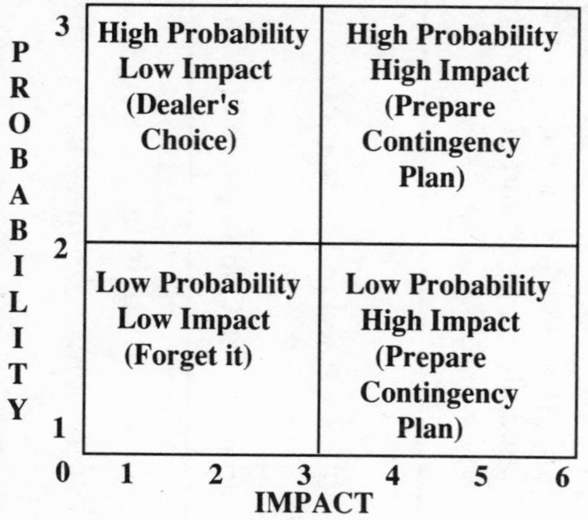

*The Contingency Plan responds to the Risk Situation.

**The Preventive Plan responds to the Probable Cause(s).

Revise plans by:

- Reassigning strong staff to high-risk and critical path tasks
- Assigning a person, if only minimally, as a backup to any tasks where the loss of a team member would be damaging

Make and document backup plans including:

- Preventive actions that will be taken to reduce or remove risk
- Contingent actions that can be implemented should a problem occur
- The circumstances that would trigger each contingency plan into action

For each risk, ask the following questions and then assign a value of high, medium, or low: (1) What is the probability this risk will occur? (2) What would be the impact if this risk should occur? For risks with high rankings for either impact or probability, take preventive steps by making revisions to the schedule or adjusting resource assignments or negotiating a contingency fund and by generating backup contingency plans. For each backup contingency plan, specify the circumstances that would trigger the plan into action (see Figure 5-22).

Contingency is essential to good project management; without it, corrective action cannot be taken when problems are encountered in the execution of the work. Keep in mind that it is not prudent to hide or bury contingency within the estimates of budgets or durations, or the budgets of the tasks. Contingency should be based on the amount of risk associated with the project, and a risk assessment must be prepared as the project plan is being developed. Some risks have the potential to affect the entire project, others might affect only one phase of it, and still others might affect only a single task. Your goal should be to return the contingency to the general funds of the organization at the conclusion of the project. Unexpended contingency increases the profitability of the project or the return on investment associated with the project.

# Chapter 6
# Managing Project Change

Change affects our lives dramatically, ruining our plans, causing us to destroy completed work, and forcing us to plan, replan, replan, and replan again. We work, rather consistently, to discourage it, and yet it is inevitable.

An efficient change management process can make the difference between project success and project failure. Changes to the project will inevitably occur in the baseline of the schedule, resource allocation, and budget, as well as in the scope of the end product. These changes must be analyzed, their impact determined, and corrective action taken when necessary. In this chapter, we focus on two major types of change that affect projects: scope changes and baseline changes. We discuss the different sources for each of these changes and recommend procedures for successfully managing these all-important dynamics of your project.

## Scope Changes

### Sources of Scope Changes

Changes in the scope of a project refer to the additions, modifications, or deletions made to the end product or service. In most organizations, changes in scope occur within the areas of the project requirements and design, as well as the overriding technology, business cycle, and, last but certainly not least, personnel:

- *Requirements changes:* This common type of scope change originates with the client, who may need an additional capability or feature that was not specified in the original scope definition. In most cases, clients are not attempting to cause extra work. Rather, they probably have not considered this particular feature before and now are placing great importance on including it within the scope of the project.
- *Design changes:* During the effort, the designers may find a much better way to produce or provide the end product. Usually this

type of change occurs within the natural flow of idea generation and testing. As in the case of requirements changes, designers may place great importance on including the design change within the project scope.

- *Technological changes:* As a project evolves, new types of technology in equipment, materials, or expertise may become available. These technological discoveries must be addressed in terms of changes to the original project scope.
- *Business changes:* Nothing stands still, especially time. And with the passage of time, circumstances within the business environment change. If a competitor announces a new product or the value of the dollar declines, for example, the project scope can be affected to a greater or lesser degree. There is a need for proactive response mechanisms to adjust the project scope.
- *Personnel changes:* As circumstances change, so do people. The client may leave, additional clients may be brought into the loop, or the project manager may be pulled off the project. With each of these possible changes come adjustments to project requirements, design, technology, and business perceptions.

The initiation of changes in scope due to any of these sources must be tracked and evaluated by employing a sound change control procedure. If change control is not in place, you become so involved in taking care of bits and pieces that the original project outcomes (time, dollar, and/or resource baselines) cannot be achieved as planned. Once baselines start slipping, questions arise that you must address in terms of proving who is responsible for the overages caused by the scope changes. To cope with these issues, you need a mechanism for change control.

### Procedures for Managing Scope Changes

Scope changes have an enormous impact on the project because they deal with the end product or end service. Change control procedures should be based on three objectives to facilitate efficient and effective scope changes:

### Key Objectives for Change Control

1. To define what the project manager can and cannot do when a change of scope occurs
2. To establish an agreed-upon process for submitting the change and evaluating its impact on the current project baseline
3. To show how to approve and disapprove—based on sound business premises—the time, effort, and dollars required for the change

Five major steps are necessary for accomplishing these three objectives.

*Step 1:* Either you as project manager or the person requesting the change of scope completes the section of the change control form (Figure 6-1) that describes the change (what) and its benefits (why). We suggest that the person requesting the change complete this section since he or she is most familiar with the full scope of the request. In some cases (for example, within politically sensitive project environments), the project manager may need to complete the form and reconfirm with the client.

*Step 2:* The change controller (the project manager or a team member) assigns the document a change number, indicates the date the change control form was received, and logs the change control request on a change control log (Figure 6-2), which documents the change control number, the date submitted, a short description of the change, and the department and telephone number of the person requesting the change. The change controller then places this change on the agenda for the change control committee to address in Step 3.

*Step 3:* The change control committee is composed of members from the technical and the business arenas, as well as a decision maker from the organization who will be paying for the investigation and implement-

**Figure 6-1.** Change control form.

**PART 1 -- REQUESTER**

Name:______________________ Department: ______________________

Extension: ______________________ Date: ______________________

Description of change:

Benefits:

**PART 2 -- CHANGE CONTROLLER**

Change Number:______________________ Date Received:______________________

**PART 3 -- CHANGE CONTROL COMMITTEE**

Disposition:______________________ (Cancel or continue) Date:______________

______________________ ______________________ ______________________

BUSINESS PROJECT MANAGER (if applicable) BUSINESS MANAGER TECHNICAL PROJECT MANAGER (if applicable)

**PART 4 -- INVESTIGATION TEAM**

Assigned to: ______________________ Date: ______________________

Impact:

**PART 5 -- APPROVAL COMMITTEE**

Disposition:______________________ (Cancel or continue)

Date: ______________________ Priority: ______________________

______________________ ______________________

DEPARTMENT MANAGER BUSINESS/PROJECT MANAGER

______________________ ______________________

TECHNICAL PROJECT MANAGER (if applicable) BUSINESS MANAGER

**Figure 6-2.** Change control log.

| CHANGE CONTROL NUMBER | DATE SUBMITTED | DESCRIPTION OF CHANGE | DEPARTMENT | TELEPHONE EXTENSION | DATE REQUIRED | EFFORT EXERTED | STATUS |
|---|---|---|---|---|---|---|---|
| | | | | | | | |
| | | | | | | | |
| | | | | | | | |
| | | | | | | | |
| | | | | | | | |
| | | | | | | | |
| | | | | | | | |
| | | | | | | | |
| | | | | | | | |
| | | | | | | | |
| | | | | | | | |
| | | | | | | | |
| | | | | | | | |
| | | | | | | | |
| | | | | | | | |
| | | | | | | | |

ing the requested change. The committee should meet frequently to review pending change control forms and to decide whether the change of scope warrants further action by the investigation team. If the change of scope is canceled, the procedure stops here. If the change of scope is deemed worthy of further investigation, the committee agrees to its funding. The members sign and date the change control form and assign it to the appropriate individuals who will perform Step 4. The change controller then updates the change control log, noting the approval date for the change control investigation and to whom it has been assigned.

*Step 4:* The investigation team, which may be comprised of the same members as the change control committee, analyzes the impact this change of scope will have on the project and makes appropriate recommendations. The length of this team's investigation varies according to the nature of the change requested. The team may find that the impact will be to lengthen the target date, to require additional resources, to extend the budget, to have political ramifications, or to place the organization in a position of jeopardy. These impacts suggest negative implications, but this is not always the case. A change of scope can have a positive impact, such as shortening the duration of the project or improving the end product. Keep in mind that scope changes submitted early in the project life cycle are more likely to have less negative impact upon the baseline. In other words, if the change is requested during the design effort, there will probably be fewer adverse effects than if the change surfaces during production/development. The investigation team completes its assessment and returns the change control form to the change controller, who is then responsible for getting the request on the agenda for the next approval committee meeting (Step 5).

*Step 5:* The approval committee is made up of the same members as the change control committee with the possible addition of other appropriate decision makers. This committee evaluates the potential impact of the scope change, as reported by the investigation team, and decides whether to approve the request. The decision should take into consideration not only the positions of each of the individual contributing departments, but also the impact on the organization as a whole. If a change is approved, the approval committee may also set priorities as well as sign off on the document. The project manager is given a copy, and the change controller completes the log designating approval or disapproval, the date, and to whom the work has been assigned.

This procedure is appropriate for large changes of scope that have major ramifications for the project but can be too formal for small, seemingly insignificant or discrete change requests. An alternative is a one-page document that describes the change of scope requested and compares the current expected completion date, effort exerted, project personnel, and project costs with the changes that would occur in these areas if the change of scope were implemented (Figure 6-3). There is space in the document for recommendations and for signatures of appropriate personnel. If only one line is required to document the change of scope, a change control log sheet (Figure 6-2), describing who made the request for the change of scope, who approved it, who accomplished it, and the impact of the change, is adequate.

## Baseline Changes

### Sources of Baseline Changes

Now let's look at the ways in which you and the project team can identify and properly record all requirements to change the project baseline. *Project baseline* specifically refers to the project specifications, applicable standards, schedule target, cost target, and resource and asset utilization targets. Baseline changes, which deal with the project plan, are easier to anticipate than scope changes because they can be tracked against actual performance by the project manager, functional manager, and team members.

There are four primary sources of baseline changes to the project (Figure 6-4): client driven, regulatory driven, externally driven, and internally driven, each with a number of different subtypes. Some types of change commonly occur and can be identified and acted upon very quickly. Others are far more subtle and can sneak up on the project team, causing unacceptable cost increases and schedule delays.

In some organizations, the project team is responsible for monitoring the potential for change from various sources. Other organizations have work units established specifically to monitor sources of change and alter the project plans when something is afoot that might affect them. In Chapters 7 and 8, we discuss how these baseline changes can be monitored through project control concepts and techniques, respectively. For now, let's take a closer look at each of these four sources of baseline changes and their accompanying subtypes.

#### Client Driven

The client is the owner, or future owner, of the product being developed by the project team. You need to know who the client is—and who is authorized to speak for the client in dealing with the project team.

Client-driven change occurs for a variety of reasons, but there are three basic interrelated issues for it:

1. *Scope:* All facets of the end product are of concern to the client. At any time during the project cycle, the client may alter the

**Figure 6-3.** Project review chart.

Project Name _____  Project Number _____  Starting Date _____

Status: ☐ No Revisions  ☐ Revisions Included  ☐ Postimplementation Audit  ☐ Other: _____

Phase Completed: ☐ Project Outline  ☐ Detail Design
☐ Concept Design  ☐ Development/Testing

| Present | Completion Date | Person-Months | Project Personnel | Project Cost |
|---|---|---|---|---|
|  |  |  |  |  |

Changes to Scope of Project or Revisions to Previous Estimates

| Revised | Completion Date | Person-Months | Project Personnel | Project Cost |
|---|---|---|---|---|
|  |  |  |  |  |

Changes from Previous Estimates

Recommendation

_____  _____  _____
Department Head's Signature                              Title                              Date

☐ Approved  ☐ Disapproved
Reason (if any) _____

Signature _____  Date _____

**Figure 6-4.** Sources of change to the baseline.

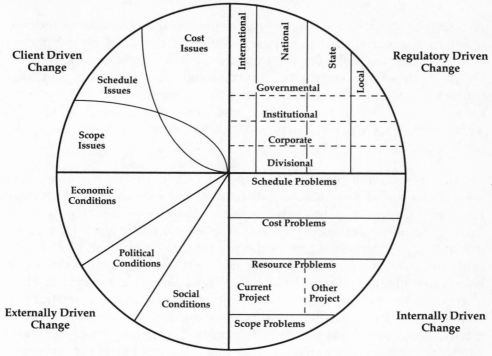

characteristics of the end product by initiating a change to the scope. (When we talk about scope changes here, we are focusing on baseline changes that are brought about by the client's desire to alter the characteristics of the end product.)

2. *Cost:* The client is concerned with total cost as well as periodic cost (fiscal year, quarter). The client may find it necessary to alter either, thereby changing the baselines given to the project team. While it is most common to think in terms of reducing the cost of the project, the client may sometimes seek to increase the cost. For example, the client may be faced with a budgetary surplus for a quarter and may want to increase the cost of the project during that quarter as a means of dealing with the surplus. The client may be looking at cost exclusively or at cost-schedule relationships.

3. *Schedule:* The client is often concerned with completion dates and with interim milestone dates. For a variety of reasons, the client may seek to alter these delivery dates. While it is most common to deal with a client who is seeking to advance the date(s), it is not unheard of to receive a request to delay the delivery of the end product, often for cost-related reasons.

### Regulatory Driven

Regulatory-driven changes originate with organizations or individuals having the authority to impose mandatory directives on the project team. It is best to think of regulatory change as a matrix (see Figure 6-4). On one side of the matrix are international, national, state, and local sources of change. On the other side are governmental, quasi-governmental or institutional, corporate, and divisional sources of change. Thus, there is a sixteen-cell matrix of potential regulatory changes to the project baseline.

1. *Governmental change:* The top left cell of the matrix is governmental change of an international nature. For example, the European Economic Community recently instituted changes in the requirements for registering pharmaceuticals, a change that directly affects the growing number of project teams in the pharmaceutical industry. The next cell, national governmental change, may be the most obvious source of regulatory change, but it is also the most complex because a large number of federal government regulations affect many organizations. A common question regarding national govenmental regulations is whether a particular agency has the right to regulate certain types of work and production effort. Obviously, the answers are as varied as the types and natures of the regulations within particular industries.

Many state governments duplicate and expand upon these national regulatory functions. For example, project teams in environmental industries frequently deal with the federal Environmental Protection Agency as well as a state equivalent, such as the Department of Environmental Quality. The most common example of local government regulations is building codes. These codes typically vary from municipality to municipality and must be complied with by project teams in or affiliated with the construction industry.

2. *Institutional change:* The next row of cells deals with institutional or quasi-governmental (affiliated with the government) regulators that affect the project baseline. The first cell in this row encompasses international institutional regulators. One of the most prominent examples is the International Consultative Committee on Telephony and Telegraphy (ICCTT), which sets hardware and software standards for voice and data communications that *all* telephone companies and most communications corporations must comply with. The next cell deals with national institutional regulators, such as the Underwriters Laboratories, Inc., a profit-making corporation of the American Society for Testing and Materials (ASTM), which is a quasi-governmental agency. The third cell refers to state institutional regulators, such as Connecticut's Historical Preservation Society, which may have an impact on the construction project plans of corporations or homeowners. The final cell in this row contains local

institutional regulators, such as the architectural control boards established by a number of cities or local zoning commissions that determine what use may be made of the land within a municipality.

3. *Corporate change:* The third row of cells deals with corporate regulators. The number of relevant cells in this row depends on the size and global reach of the corporation. The first cell in this row refers to international corporate regulations that emanate from the organization's world headquarters. In the second cell are national corporate regulations—those issued by the office responsible for all operations of the corporation within the country. The third cell includes regulations of the local operating unit of the corporation, such as a division. Regulations that come from the plant or facility in which the project team is situated comprise the remaining cell in this row.

4. *Divisional change:* The final row of cells in the regulatory matrix refers to the division or strategic business unit in which the project team is located. The four cells of international, national, state, and local regulations are crossed with the appropriate business unit.

Not all of these regulatory cells will affect every project. The project team should first identify the cells with the potential to affect the project baseline and then monitor any regulatory changes.

### Externally Driven

Externally driven change emanates from the environment in which the project team's organization operates. There are three types of environmental change that can affect the project: economic, political, and social. Economic change can affect the way the project progresses rather than the end product itself. For example, the baseline of a hardware project may change because the cost of computer chips has tripled over the recent quarter or the chips are not available. Politically driven change might be caused by an event or circumstance that alters the customer or consumer environment for the organization (e.g., the impact of the *Valdez* oil spill on Exxon). Finally, there is socially driven change—for example, when it became unacceptable for businesses to have dealings with the Republic of South Africa.

### Internally Driven

Internally driven changes are typically forces on the project team because of altered conditions or problems within the organization. There are several different types of change within this general area:

1. *Change necessitated by scope or technical problems:* For example, a project team may have difficulty meeting the technical objectives

of the project due to organizationwide changes in information systems processing. The team therefore may need to make technical modifications. If the organization is unable to deliver a product that meets technical objectives, the client should be approached in an attempt to change the scope of the project.

2. *Change necessitated by problems in meeting the schedule:* These problems may be associated with or independent of resource considerations. Regardless of the source, when an organization knows that it cannot meet the delivery date for an end product, renegotiating the project baseline with the client is appropriate and necessary.

3. *Change because of cost problems:* When an organization forecasts that the cost at completion of a project will exceed the maximum amount the client is willing to invest, the baseline must be altered.

4. *Change because of resource demands:* Either other projects and/or work units or the project team may be creating excessive demands for resources that the organization cannot accommodate. In either case, the schedule and/or the cost baseline of the project will more than likely have to be renegotiated.

### Procedures for Managing Baseline Changes

As much as we would like to think of baselines as static, they are not. They will change as the project evolves because of these various reasons:

### Sources of Baseline Changes

- Time targets will not be met.
- Tasks will slip their deadlines.
- Milestones will be missed.
- Jobs won't always get started on time.
- Resources will not be available as planned.
- Equipment capacity will be overestimated.
- People will not produce at peak performance.
- Budgets will be either overspent or underspent (depending on the degree of adherence to the schedule and resource allocations).
- Work accomplishment will exceed or not meet with the plan.

There are three general steps for managing baseline changes, and they will help you manage your time more efficiently:

*Step 1:* Ensure that baseline changes are committed to by one person—you! As project manager, you are the focal point for all changes because you have total perspective or overview of the project and can evaluate the total impact of the change on the balance of the project baseline. In some cases, you must approve the change. In other cases, you merely must be informed of it.

*Step 2:* There is some discussion as to whether project managers should be informed of every change or just of changes that will have an important impact on the project. For example, if a task that has three weeks of float is going to slip two days, do you have to be informed? Probably not. However, project team members should know the point at which you must be informed of baseline changes. This information should be communicated to you before the slippage in the task creates a new critical path. If there is any concern that uncontrollable baseline changes may occur, then follow this rule: *All changes must be automatically communicated to the project manager.*

*Step 3:* Tracking baseline changes can be a laborious, time-consuming effort. As a result, establish rules for timing the submission of them. For example, they should be submitted at specified times (e.g., each Tuesday morning) or discussed at biweekly status review meetings. Discourage project team members from calling or writing to you whenever they wish to announce baseline changes.

Track baseline changes for three reasons: to wave red flags, to document and analyze problems, and to negotiate for assistance in the most effective way. When your project gets into a crisis, do not hesitate to address baseline changes. It is time-consuming to rework the plans, reissue them, and deal with the questions as to why the baselines are not consistent with the plan. However, this is the juncture at which you as a project manager need to take a bold, calculated view of reality and its impact on the balance of the project.

Establish your own baseline change procedure by following these guidelines:

### Key Guidelines for Establishing a Baseline Change Procedure

- The person who is responsible for processing baseline changes should also coordinate the change among project team members.
- Attempt to make baseline changes on a scheduled basis rather than at random.
- Do not ignore the formal baseline change process when the project gets into a crisis.
- Communicate the changes that have been made to various levels, the rest of the team members, and the client.

- Establish predefined authority and approval points. For example, you can authorize slippage in a task as long as it has float, but go to the client before slipping the entire project completion date.
- Define reserves in time, resources, or dollars.
- Allow changes to be made by authorized personnel only. The functional manager can authorize a change in personnel, but a team member can't arbitrarily trade off with someone else.
- Consider possible side effects before approving any change.
- Study alternatives. Work within the constraints given. Ask for trade-offs only when absolutely necessary.
- Don't be afraid to change the baseline when necessary.
- Don't overreact. Wait for the baseline change to take effect and its impact to be evaluated before implementing another change.
- Document the change thoroughly: when it was made, why, and by whom it was approved. This will help explain the rationale of decisions later and will help build a better history base for future reference.
- Track the change to ensure that there are no unanticipated ramifications.

# Chapter 7
# A Model for Project Control

In this chapter, we address an old project management adage: "Plan the work—now work the plan." Once a project has been properly defined, carefully worded in a scope document, and detailed according to a plan, you as project manager enter into what is commonly referred to as the project management control cycle. The key questions you must answer now are: Where are we? Where do we want to be? How do we get there? Are we getting there?

In more technical terms, the question "Where are we?" asks for an assessment of the current status of the project. "Where do we want to be?" asks for a comparison of the actual progress made against the baseline project plan. "How do we get there?" asks for a consideration of possible corrective actions that could put the project back on track, if necessary, or help keep it there. And "Are we getting there?" asks for an analysis of the impact these corrective actions will have or are having on the project.

We first look at the transition between the planning process and the controlling process. Next, we discuss the differences between formal and informal control, which leads into a discussion of what specifically belongs in a controlling model. We also provide a series of guidelines to support the five stages of the controlling process: updating the status, analyzing the impact, acting on the variances, publishing the revisions, and informing management.

The last part of the chapter discusses "who": who should be responsible for what parts of the controlling process. The team members, of course, have a role within the process. What is that role? And is there a rationale for employing project control specialists? What might they contribute to this process?

## Transition From Planning to Controlling

A project manager does not stop planning at 5 P.M. one day and commence controlling the next morning at 9 A.M. without orchestrating the environment so that the project can be managed—that is, so that the relevant parties are involved and aware of the rules. Four steps belong on your transition checklist:

## Transition Steps From Planning to Controlling

1. Validate plans.
2. Obtain sign-offs and freeze plans.
3. Resell the benefits of project management.
4. Create a project notebook.

*Step 1: Validate plans.* Before issuing the final set of plans, ensure that the plans appear to be reasonable. Figure 7-1 provides a list of items you may want to consider. Add more items as you see fit. Validating plans also includes updating status since work on the project may have commenced prior to the completion of the planning.

*Step 2: Obtain sign-offs and freeze plans.* Sign-off procedures are a very important part of the process. More than likely, there will be questions

**Figure 7-1.** Validation of plans: project management system, general purpose.

| Project Name | | Project Number | | Page | of |
|---|---|---|---|---|---|
| Prepared by | | Date | | New ☐ | Revised ☐ |

**Planning Checklist**

| | yes | no | | yes | no |
|---|---|---|---|---|---|
| Are maximum of three tasks assigned per person per week? | — | — | Actual start? Actual completion? | | |
| Is task limited to 40-80 effort hours? | — | — | Will project team members receive a work schedule weekly? | | |
| Is there deliverable output for each task? | — | — | | — | — |
| Do tasks relate to objectives? | — | — | Is a master plan to be maintained? Who will maintain it? | — | — |
| Have completion criteria been established for each task? | — | — | | | |
| Have tasks been reviewed with project team members? | — | — | Is total plan duration limited to project phase of 6 months (or reasonable horizon)? | — | — |
| Do project team members agree on: | | | Have tasks been included for: | | |
| task estimated effort? | — | — | Preparation? | — | — |
| task planned start date? | — | — | Walk throughs? | — | — |
| task planned completion date? | — | — | Revisions? | — | — |
| Is one person responsible for each task? | — | — | Does every task have a person assigned? | — | — |
| Have all tasks needed to accomplish objectives been included in the plan? | — | — | Is task effectiveness rate 60 percent or greater? | — | — |
| Are estimated efforts within boundaries of task elapsed time? | — | — | Has original or revised plan been approved by Project Manager, Division Head, and Department Head? | — | — |
| Is overtime scheduled? | — | — | Are the following types of plans prepared and complete? | | |
| Does a network diagram exist? | — | — | Resource plan? | — | — |
| | | | Financial (cost) plan? | — | — |
| Do project team members agree to record the following data weekly: | | | Data processing resource requirements plan? | — | — |
| Actual effort? | — | — | Test plan? | — | — |
| Forecasted effort? | — | — | Training plan? | — | — |

from those who must approve the plan. There will be fewer questions if you have involved all the parties during the development of the plan; formatted the plan as clearly and as professionally as possible; set up a formalized approval process; provided time for approval; and communicated, communicated, communicated.

In many organizations it is difficult to get clients, functional managers, and even team members to sign off or to freeze the plans. They are afraid that their signature will be held as a club over their head. If they change their minds, they see the plan, now frozen, as an impediment. Explain that an approved plan as the baseline is a prerequisite to controlling a project. Remember that the baseline is valid at the moment it is approved; is not set in concrete; should be considered a flexible management tool; is the basis for a warning signal of potential problems looming ahead; and can be renegotiated with the proper documentation and professional presentation.

*Step 3: Resell the benefits of project management.* At this point in the project's evolution, it may be important to resell the benefits of project management. Those involved have slogged their way through technical and political issues in order to produce the plan; they have exerted time and effort, and finally the long-awaited moment has arrived for the project to get underway—at least the meaningful part of the project, which in their minds is the design and development of the end product. They may need encouragement that all their effort was not wasted and that these plans will help support them during the upcoming control process. The following benefits may help sustain that buy-in and commitment:

### Benefits of the Project Plan for the Control Cycle

- The plan ensures that no major tasks have been forgotten.
- The plan indicates clearly the assignment of responsibility, accountability, and authority.
- The plan predefines the interdependencies of tasks one to another, and thus functional interdependencies as well.
- The plan becomes a yardstick against which to measure status and, ultimately, to judge the success or failure of the project, the project manager, and the project team members.
- The plan, which will now be used as a monitoring, tracking, and controlling tool, becomes a vehicle for communication and control.

*Step 4: Create a project notebook.* If you have not already done this, take some time before the controlling process begins to organize the project notebook. Set aside sections for the project definition, communication plan, task descriptions (work breakdown structure), estimates of each task and the background rationale, an ongoing list of assumptions, an ongoing history log of change control and baseline changes, status reports, and project summary (which will be produced at the end of the project).

## Formal and Informal Control

The project plan is complete. It has been presented to senior management (and perhaps a client) and has been approved. Work on the project is about to commence. It is time to ensure that the change management procedure is in place and being adhered to by both client and project team. And it is time to define how you will control the work during the project's execution.

A common belief is that formal project control, which includes status reporting at the end of a week, month, or accounting period, is the most effective means of controlling the project's progress. This is not the case. The most effective control is exercised daily (or almost daily) through your interaction with project team members. A formal control, at the close of a week, month, or accounting period, serves other purposes.

### Performing Informal Project Control

Informal control is not a new idea. For years, construction project managers have walked the job, observed work in process, and talked to the personnel doing this work. In 1982, Tom Peters and Bob Waterman popularized the concept, which they labeled "management by wandering around," in their book, *In Search of Excellence*.[1] Informal control has a number of benefits:

#### Benefits of Informal Control

- You learn a lot more than you do by sitting at your desk.
- You meet people in their habitat, where they may be more open and honest than they are in your office or a conference room.
- You are highly visible to all project staff, not just your direct subordinates. You are more of a team member.
- Your team will be delighted to explain their latest successful efforts.

[1] *In Search of Excellence: Lessons from America's Best-Run Companies* (New York: Warner Books, 1982).

> Nothing begets success like success. The more you make them feel good about their accomplishments, the more they will try to accomplish.
> - You learn of brewing problems faster than waiting for them to appear on a status report or in a meeting.
> - You develop a sixth sense for what is normal within the team and then can discern potential problems.

There is one caution: resist the urge to micro-manage by giving direction on the spot or skipping a level of management by making decisions that are the responsibility of someone else in the project team. You undermine the project organization you yourself established and give mixed messages to the project team as to whom they are to follow.

Under most circumstances, informal control should be performed on a daily basis or as close to it as possible given your schedule. Informal control is the interaction between you and your team members, during which you have an increased awareness of the project's current condition, in addition to items that need immediate attention. If you do not have time to perform informal project control, then the project will suffer.

As you interact with your team, its members can ask questions and present problems. Informal control should have the effect of increasing the team's accessibility to you.

When performing informal control, you are forming a mental image of the project's status or condition and comparing this image to the project plan. You are also forming a mental image of the project's future: a forecast that is used to determine if the project is in trouble in any way. From this mental comparison, you can determine if there is a need for corrective and/or preventive actions.

Corrective and/or preventive actions may be taken as part of the process of informal control. As you work with project team members, solicit potential solutions to current problems, evaluate them with the team, and take any necessary action. Furthermore, you can use informal control as a means of evaluating the effectiveness of previously implemented solutions to problems. The image of the project's condition that you form during informal control is carried over to the formal control process.

Your accessibility is the key to informal control. If you are inaccessible, you won't learn of issues that are in need of attention.

### Performing Formal Project Control

Formal project control is a newer concept than informal control, and it's more of a paper than a mental exercise. Formal control can be performed by week, month, or accounting period through the use of project reports. Be careful that you don't perform formal control too frequently, since the time and effort involved in it can prevent you from performing frequent informal control.

In formal project control, you are gathering data about recently completed tasks as well as in-process tasks. These data are used to produce status reports that indicate project performance up to the control cycle cutoff date and to prepare analysis or forecast reports based on experiences in performing the work to date.

These status and analysis reports can serve as the basis for negotiating preventive and corrective actions in dealing with problems being experienced in the execution of the work. Once the required preventive or corrective actions have been taken, status and analysis reports incorporating those actions are used as the basis for preparing summary senior management and client reports. Thus, the periodic reports give you the information necessary to keep all concerned parties informed of the project's condition.

### Formal and Informal Control: A Comparison

The steps in formal and informal control processes are the same: data are collected concerning recently completed tasks as well as tasks underway; status reports (historical in nature) are prepared either mentally or on paper and are used to forecast future performance on the project; these forecasts form the basis for determining the need for corrective or preventive actions, which are then negotiated between project manager and project team members, and possibly with the client.

The most obvious differences between formal and informal control are medium, effort, and frequency. The **medium** for informal control is the mind (although with user-friendly microcomputer-based project management software, often project managers make copies of the most recent plans and assess the impact of variances on the screen as well as in the mind).

The **effort** associated with informal and formal control depends in part on the state of the project. In both types of control, less effort is required if the project is in good condition and being accomplished in accordance with the plan. If the project is in trouble, more effort is required by both project manager and team. The monthly effort associated with informal control can be measured in minutes per day. Monthly effort connected with formal control is measured in hours per month, with most of the work occurring shortly after the close of the formal reporting period. In reality, informal control may require as much effort as formal control or even more, but the effort is spread out.

**Frequency** of informal control can be determined by the project manager, depending on time constraints and the general condition of the project. In most cases, it will occur daily or almost daily. The frequency of formal control is determined by management and the client, who dictate the intervals between the formal status reports they expect to receive. In most cases, the formal control period is by month or accounting period.

In order to reconcile the results of formal and informal control, compare the status and analysis reports to the mental image of the project condition you have formed during informal control. The reports and the image should be consistent with each other, and there should be no surprises in the formal status and analysis reports. If there are, you need to increase the frequency of informal control.

### Relative Effectiveness of Formal and Informal Control

To determine the relative effectiveness of formal and informal control, it is necessary to make several assumptions. Let's consider a case in which the organization performs formal control on a monthly basis and the project manager, who has a wide range of responsibilities, performs informal control only once every three or four days. Assume that these broad responsibilities make it difficult for project team members to get the project manager's attention other than during formal or informal control interactions.

A problem in performing project work occurs on the sixth working day of the period. The team member experiencing this problem has previously met with frustration in trying to contact the project manager. Therefore, the team member makes no attempt now to communicate directly and immediately with the project manager.

Under the formal control scenario, the project manager learns of the problem in the status report for the current period, which (optimistically) is prepared on the fifth working day of the next period. In that case, somewhere between twenty-seven and thirty calendar days have passed between the onset of the problem and the project manager's awareness of it. During that period, if the project manager is lucky, the problem has not become worse. On the other hand, the situation may have become considerably worse. The team member has been trying to solve the problem but lacks the necessary authority and resources. Now that the problem has finally been brought to the attention of the project manager, it will be dealt with effectively—but at higher cost in money and resources.

Under informal control, the project manager learns of the problem within one to three days after the team member has discovered it and can immediately exert some authority and resources to solve the problem. Since the problem has had little time to ripen, dealing with it may not be costly. The impact of the problem on the end date and cost at completion of the project will be less, and the organization will be better off because the problem has been solved in less time and at lower cost.

Both informal and formal control processes are needed, but informal can be much more important to effective project management.

### Creating a Sense of Importance and Consequence

As you employ both the formal and the informal project control approaches, be sure to create a sense of importance and consequence from the very beginning of the project. We know that on Day 1, eighteen months looks like a long way off. However, if you are complacent about getting the project done, the rest of the team will be, too. You can generate a sense of urgency in several ways:

#### Ways to Generate a Sense of Urgency

- Have a high level of focused energy from Day 1.
- Let the team know you are looking at the big picture as well as details.
- Hurry to get ahead (don't wait to catch up).
- Hold frequent staff meetings at which you exhibit this sense of importance and consequence.
- Hold daily meetings as needed where the action is.
- Give a firm time limit for problem solution.
- Post schedules, highlighting slippages in prominent, visible areas for all to see.

Performing formal and informal control is not an either-or situation. Both are required for effective project management. But remember that they serve different purposes. Problems surface quickly with informal control, which affords the opportunity to deal with them before they ripen. Formal control checks the adequacy of informal control and confirms what the project manager already knows about the project. It is the basis of developing and delivering summary status reports for senior management and the client. To be successful as a project manager, you must do both, and do them well.

## A Five-Step Model for Project Control

Tracking and managing the project means taking steps to ensure that actual performance conforms to the project plan. The basic tools for controlling the project are the project definition (which serves as a contract for measuring the success of the project, the end product, and the project manager); the project plan, schedule, resource plan, and budget; and status reports, which indicate work in progress and problems. The project plan serves as a road map for the project team's efforts; it sets expectations. Your job is to see that those expectations are met. Let's look at each of the five stages in the controlling process:

### Five-Step Model for Project Control

---

1. Update the status.
2. Analyze the impact.
3. Act on the variances.
4. Publish the revisions.
5. Inform management.

---

### Step 1: Update the Status

Use the systems you've put into place to track work accomplishment and costs and to assess the quality of the work being done. Also look at the morale and productivity of the project team. Your job as the project manager during the controlling process is to concentrate on the progress of the schedule, costs, quality, human resource allocation, fixed costs, materials, and supplies.

Updating the status focuses on collecting the information necessary to assess performance on the project and posting the information. The data, collected from the members of the project team, the cost accounting system, and the time reporting system, are then posted so that they can be compared to the plan. The nature of the posting process depends on the manual or automated project management system being used.

Data requirements vary; completed tasks, tasks in process, and future tasks each must be examined somewhat differently. The schedule, resource utilization, cost, and achievement status reports are produced as a result of the updating. Let's first discuss mechanisms for collecting data and then how to decide the form and substance of status reports.

#### Confirm or Set Up Mechanisms for Collecting Data

Mechanisms need to be in place to collect data for schedules, deliverables, costs, and problems. This information can come from several sources:

## Sources for Collecting Data

- *Project manager interviews:* The project manager interviews each member of the team to determine the status of the tasks to which each member is assigned.
- *Person holding prime responsibility:* Task owners update the project baselines for which they are accountable and submit them to the project manager, who then prepares a consolidated project status report.
- *Status review meetings:* All members of the team inform the project manager and each other of tasks begun, tasks completed, tasks behind schedule, and any potential problems.
- *Personnel time reports, time cards, or time logs:* Project team members fill out the reports. The data are correlated and consolidated in a master status report.

These four sources do not excuse you from walking around or from maintaining one-on-one communication. If there is no mechanism in place, you must develop a medium for collecting data. If you design your own data collection forms:

- Make them simple and easy to complete.
- Ensure that all the information is pertinent.
- Confirm that those preparing the information understand how it will be utilized and the need for their input.
- Make sure people are aware of its end use.
- Make sure there are consistent "as-of" dates.

### Decide on Status Reporting Forms

In order to keep everyone informed, you will issue status reports. A number of key questions need to be answered when making decisions concerning these reports:

## Questions for Status Reports

- What will they look like? Graphic or lists? Narrative or pictures?
- Who will be on the distribution list?
- Who will receive differing levels of detail?
- How frequently will the reports be issued?

> - What will the reports be used for (merely for communication? as the basis for progress reporting meetings? as action tools to manage the project?)?
> - What image do you want to portray?
> - How easy is it to update the reports? (The easier, the better.)

There is a good rule of thumb: Project team members at a lower level of detail require data on a more frequent basis and usually prefer a list format. Management prefers graphs presented to them on a less frequent basis with a short executive summary and at a higher level of detail (see Table 7-1). Team members need information different from that given to management:

## Information for Project Team Members on Status Reports

> - What you want them to do
> - What authority you have delegated to them
> - What results you expect
> - What help they will have
> - What rewards (consequences) they will be given

**Table 7-1.** Status reporting decisions.

| | Top Management | Immediate Supervisors | Team Members |
|---|---|---|---|
| **Levels of Detail** | Less detail, more graphic, information tool | Intermediate | Greater detail, lists, action tool |
| **Timing** | Less frequently (minimum monthly) | Intermediate | More frequently (minimum weekly) |
| **Content** | Just the overview, problem isolation, and recommendations | Everything that is produced | Only the sections that affect them |

**Information for Management on Status Reports**

- Where you are
- Where you should be
- Where you are going next
- How you are going to get there
- What resources are needed
- When you are going to get there

When documenting any status report, determine who is taking responsibility for what: Who is collecting the data? Who is correlating the data? Who ensures that the data are credible? Who produces the reports? Who distributes them? Be sure each report is communicating the information that audience needs to know—no more and no less. Also, be sure you choose a format and level of detail appropriate to your audience. Finally, make reporting techniques as flexible as possible for easy updating.

### Step 2: Analyze the Impact

Step 2 is subdivided into three parts:

1. Compare planned to actual results in order to reveal variance. This part requires that several questions be answered for each task and for the whole project: Are we ahead or behind schedule? Are we over or under budget? Are we using the staff's time as planned? Given actual staffing levels, are we getting the results we expected?
2. Determine cause. That is, when problems appear, look carefully to find the cause. Typical causes include poorly defined objectives, an incomplete or ineffective plan, inadequate communication, poor estimates, changes of scope, and staff problems. Whatever the cause of the problem is, analyze its impact on the project schedule and budget, the project team's morale, and the quality of the project deliverables.
3. Prepare analysis or forecast reports in which prior progress, or the lack thereof, is extrapolated to the future. The analysis reports indicate the forecasted completion date, the forecasted resource utilization at completion, and the forecasted final cost.

You can use this information by comparing it to senior management or client expectations for the project. If the comparison is favorable, no further action is required. If the comparisons are unfavorable, you need to take corrective action and/or preventive action.

The solving of problems in an efficient and effective manner is a logical and orderly process. One systematic approach can be stated as a series of seven steps:

### Seven Steps in Problem Solving*

1. Define the problem.
2. Collect all the pertinent data.
3. Determine all possible alternative solutions.
4. Analyze and evaluate alternatives.
5. Select the best alternative(s).
6. Implement the action decided upon.
7. Follow up to be sure the action is carried out.

1. *Define the problem.* One of the major problems of business today is that there are too many people who are running around with answers looking for problems that the answers will fit. A brilliant answer to the wrong problem is not very productive. Of all the steps in this process, defining the problem is perhaps the most difficult and certainly the most critical. Inaccuracy at this point will not only prevent solving of the real problem but may well tend to make the matter worse.

Frequently the most apparent problem is only a symptom of a far greater problem. We can choose to keep on treating symptoms, or we can exercise our intelligence and get at the heart of the problem. The real test in problem definition is in the identification of the basic cause. We must be willing to probe and dig to find the real problems, which are not always apparent. For example, alcohol is rarely the problem of alcoholics; the basic problem is generally the condition that makes them turn to alcohol as an escape. If we simply took alcohol away, we might be able to stop their drinking, but sooner or later they would find another means of escape because they are still confronted with the basic cause of their drinking. We quickly lose confidence in doctors who merely treat symp-

*A number of people suggest that items 1 and 2 be reversed. Their logic is that you cannot define the problem until the facts are known. However, it is difficult to collect pertinent data if the problem has not been defined. In reality, we do collect data prior to the definition of a problem, but once the problem has been defined, then we must review the information we have and sort out the facts. It is this final screening and selection process that is implied in Step 2.

toms, and we also lose confidence in managers who fail to probe for the basic cause.

These are only a few of the problems that project managers encounter when trying to control a project:

- *Personality conflicts:* All people do not automatically like all other people. There are barriers based on education, upbringing, political posturing, and just plain bad chemistry.
- *Poorly defined project objectives:* If the objectives are incorrect or ambiguous, the work efforts may be misdirected or erroneous, thus causing slippages and inability to meet the plan.
- *Ever-changing external forces:* These are the fateful events that were never planned. Perhaps the equipment falls off the back end of the truck when being unloaded, or the vendor's truck is in an accident and is totaled. These point to the truth of Murphy's Law: "What can go wrong will go wrong." And in some cases, it is even worse, as Callahan's corollary says: "Murphy was an optimist."
- *Lack of historical data:* Estimating is difficult at best; however, estimates without a basis of historical data are gambles.
- *Changes of scope:* New design requests cause an impact.
- *Inefficiencies within a project:* Among them are unrealistic performance standards, calendar timing derived in a pseudoscientific fashion, skill deficiencies on the part of the project team members, the learning curve required to bring new team members up to speed, poor communication (upward and downward), and diminishing morale, which decreases further with burnout.

2. *Collect all the pertinent data.* This step is a fact-gathering process. Attempt to collect all of the available data pertinent to the problem, but be wary of gathering unrelated material, which will result only in confusing the issue or clouding it, to the point where you are no longer able to focus on the problem. This is one more reason that specific problems must be solved. If the problem has been defined clearly, then the collection of data related to this problem—and this problem alone—will be greatly simplified. The collection of pertinent material requires hard work and careful analysis, but the rewards of doing a capable job in this step of problem solving far exceed the time required.

3. *Determine all possible alternative solutions.* Once the problem has been accurately defined and all the pertinent material collected, then and only then should you begin to explore solutions. Most of us have a great tendency to jump directly from the definition of the problem to its solution. This jumping is a dangerous activity, for too often we jump in the wrong direction.

When we have defined a problem, the first solution we come up with seems almost brilliant to us. We are often sure that nothing else could possibly be as good as this first answer. We may be right, but nevertheless, often further thought results in a better solution.

One of the more dangerous things to do in this phase of problem solving is to censor your own ideas; that is, we often immediately reject any ideas that have not been tried before, that we think others may ridicule, that may cost money, that may threaten our own position, and so forth. When we impose these restrictions on ourselves, ideas will not come freely. At this point, the important thing is to think up every possible solution, no matter how strange or silly it may seem. The screening and sorting of these ideas will come later in the process. Keep an open mind when looking for alternatives.

4. *Analyze and evaluate alternatives.* This is the task of separating the wheat from the chaff. Many of the alternatives either did not meet the problem or met it only partially. You are not yet looking for the best alternative but merely examining the choices to establish which ones have merit. Now is the time for testing and questioning the alternatives to find out how they fit the problem at hand. Don't reject any alternative until it has been proved to be useless in the solution of the problem. It is here that you draw on your experience, education, judgment, and knowledge to explore the suitability of every alternative.

5. *Select the best alternative(s).* The evaluation procedure may have left you with several possible solutions still available—or none at all. In the latter case, start the procedure again from the beginning. Typically, however, several alternatives will be applicable to the solutions; it is this step that pinpoints the action that you will take. Often the final selection will be a combination of several alternatives, each supporting the other(s). Regardless of whether the process discloses one or many courses of action, the important aspect is that a selection has been made. You have made a decision in regard to which course of action is the most appropriate in your judgment.

This step can be very rapid or very time-consuming, depending on the complexity of the problem and/or the alternatives. Do not allow yourself to get into analysis paralysis—analyzing forever and never making a decision.

6. *Implement the action decided upon.* Your previous work will be nothing but a waste of valuable time unless the decision made is put to use. Something must happen somewhere if the problem is to be solved. There is no telling how many fine ideas and solutions are buried in file cabinets because the individual who spent the time developing the solution did not have the courage to put it to use. Implementation may be a gamble; you cannot always be sure the solution will work. You can take only a calculated risk that you have been careful in your selection and that the odds are on your side. Unless you take this step, the problem

will still be with you, and all of your thinking and evaluative efforts will go for nothing.

7. *Follow up to be sure action is carried out.* If you had the courage to implement the action, the whole process can still come to nothing unless you follow up to make sure that the action was implemented in the manner intended. The follow-up phase determines whether the problem will stay solved. This may be accomplished through informal control.

### Step 3: Act on the Variances

There are three courses of action as a result of comparing the plan to the actual:

1. Do nothing, either because the impact is not great enough to warrant action or because the trend is not strong enough to justify action yet.
2. Look at the plans that exist and make modifications within the schedule, resource, cost, and scope baselines to accommodate the problem.
3. Start negotiating trade-offs—perhaps time added to the schedule, additional resources, additional money, and/or a resizing of the scope of the project.

The last alternative is not often considered. Let's examine a case study to discuss how it can work.

Poor Frank. He has found himself in what appears to be an impossible situation. His position as project manager is rapidly becoming an albatross around his neck, and he is very unhappy. His relationship with his supervisor, the vice-president of marketing, is a disaster. And project management is the focal point of the problem.

Frank is a conscientious project manager. When confronted with a new project assignment, his initial plan of action is to assemble a team with the requisite skills and have them develop a detailed plan for the achievement of the project objectives. He carefully reviews inputs from the project team to ensure that the cost and schedule targets for the project are reasonable and attainable but not padded. But his supervisor constantly throws monkey wrenches into the process. At plan review time, thinking that he is motivating Frank, he ignores the carefully prepared plan and substitutes arbitrary, capricious deadlines and budgets upon Frank. "I don't care about the plan, Frank. Find a way to get it done by February 1, and keep the budget under $60,000."

After Frank had related the story to us, we asked him how he was responding to the situation. His answer was somewhat surprising: Most of the time he found a way to complete the project within the unreasonable deadline established by the vice-president and within the understated budget. That was the totality of his answer, with no explanation of how he managed to perform this feat or any mention made of the vice-president's reaction to this accomplishment.

We thought about Frank's story and how he had managed to meet the deadlines and budgets arbitrarily set by his supervisor and realized that his story revealed two problems: (1) the substantive issue of how Frank managed to complete the work within the unreasonable time frame and understated budget and (2) the problem of the perception, in the vice-president's mind, created by Frank's performance.

How can Frank manage to bring in projects in unreasonably short durations for insufficient funds? There are several possibilities. Frank might be achieving the desired results by pushing the staff to work a significant amount of overtime with no compensation. If this were the case, however, one would expect to find extremely low morale within the group, as well as a higher-than-normal rate of employee turnover. When we asked Frank if this were the case, he said that the morale of the group was high and that turnover in the unit was of no consequence.

Another possibility is that Frank is able to achieve the desired results because his initial schedules and budgets were overstated, and the deadlines and budgets set by the vice-president are reasonable. But when we examined the plans, not only did they not appear to be overstated, they were based upon industry standard estimating techniques, and the techniques were applied in a manner consistent with the directions for their use. Frank's plans were, if anything, slightly understated at the time that they were presented to the vice-president.

Finally, we hit upon a likely solution and asked Frank to show us some of the deliverables he had produced by undertaking these projects. He was reluctant to do so. Unlike most other project managers we have encountered, Frank was not proud of the results he had achieved. Further probing revealed a single reason for Frank's lack of pride in his results: He had produced a series of products that were marginally functional, extremely difficult and costly to maintain, and below his (and probably his organization's) standards.

Frank had discovered a fairly common technique for survival in an environment characterized by unreasonable deadlines and inadequate budgets: treat the technical objectives as a variable rather than a constant. If the deadline is fixed and the budget is locked in, produce the quality of product attainable within the time frame and budget rather than the quality of product stated in the specifications. Take the shortcuts that are least likely to be noticed by the client. Don't alter the appearance of the product; that is too obvious to the client. Instead, alter the internals of the product, reducing quality to achieve an on-time, on-budget performance. Gamble that no one will recognize the substandard nature of the work for some time to come.

It is important to remember that Frank was not proud of his actions or the results they had produced. He felt cornered. His reaction was a means of survival in a situation in which he could not effectively negotiate with his supervisor. As a consequence, the products were produced, the group's morale remained relatively high, but Frank became extremely unhappy with the situation. On the other hand, Frank's supervisor was very pleased. He set unreasonable and understated budgets and perceived that Frank consistently delivered in a manner that fulfilled his goals. He also perceived that his technique worked and was unaware of the problems inherent in Frank's products. He was insensitive to the problem of Frank's morale. Therefore, he continued to employ the technique of applying pressure to project managers by setting arbitrary budgets and deadlines. This lack of effective communication between Frank and the vice-president has led to a recurring cycle of problems—one that will eventually be revealed as the cost of supporting and maintaining the products is reflected in the performance of the organization.

In reality, we have two problems in this situation. The first is the policy question of whether the organization wants to treat technical objectives as a variable. If this is the case, under what circumstances and with what controls is this accomplished? What level of authority should be required to decide that the technical objectives of a project are to be altered to meet the schedule or to get it done within budget? Design to cost and design to deadline can both be useful techniques in setting technical objectives, under the right set of circumstances and with the right set of controls.

The second problem may be more difficult. It is one of lack of communication and understanding. When a project manager, in a situation similar to Frank's, finds it necessary to take extraordinary action to meet the schedule or get the job done within budget, senior management must understand that the goal has been achieved as a result of extraordinary action. The project manager must let management know how it is possible to deliver on time and on budget. If nothing else, this will force management to face up to the issue of whether the technical objectives ought to be treated as a variable.

Compromising on technical objectives to meet schedules and budgets represents a significant risk to the organization and is not a decision to be taken lightly. In most cases, it is not a decision to be made at the project manager level in the organization, and it is not a decision to be made without analysis by management. If the risks are both modest and acceptable to the organization, as well as legal and ethical, then it is the responsibility of management, not the project manager, to determine that the compromise be made.

If the forecasts are at variance with the plan, you as project manager must take action to minimize the departure from the plan. There are two types of action to be considered: corrective and preventive. *Corrective action* deals with problems that have already been experienced; *preventive action* addresses anticipated problems. The need for corrective action is revealed in the historical status reports; the need for preventive action is indicated by the forecasts.

In both corrective and preventive action, the first requirement is to determine the root cause of the problem. Then you can work with the team to develop alternative solutions, evaluate the alternatives, and select one to be implemented. If you lack the authority necessary to implement the selected solution, obtain approval for it. Once approved, the solution is implemented. Then monitor the effectiveness of the solution over time. The project manager uses contingency to implement solutions to the problems experienced in the execution of the work.

Remember not to overreact. Be sure there is a trend evident before making any major changes, but don't wait too long. Problems typically do not disappear on their own. There is an analogy that relates to this issue and offers a good piece of advice. If you have a monkey (a problem) on your back, either shoot the monkey or feed it, but never starve it. Shooting the monkey means implementing corrective action as soon as possible; in other words, solve the problem and make it go away. The second acceptable option is to feed the monkey, which means to work the problem until it is resolved. But don't ignore the monkey to the point of starving it; when you ignore a starving monkey, it dies an excruciating and raucous death. And the negative attention will be brought to the project manager's doorstep.

Keep in mind the basic review-and-revise process. The basic schedules have been prepared, the variances have been analyzed, and modifications have been determined. You and the project team are revising the basic schedules of time, resources, costs, and deliverables. While making these revisions, record the assumptions that have been made. For example, "We are going to let Task A slip because we have been told by the subcontractor that he doesn't need the product from us on the delivery date; a one-week delay will not affect his turnaround time." It is important to record these assumptions, not only to be able to refer to them if there is contention at a later date but also to preserve them as part of the database you will use in planning projects in the future.

### Step 4: Publish the Revisions

It is a rare month in which there are no revisions to the project plan. Since the plan is the working document that the project team relies on for guidance, it should be updated constantly. Most corrective and preventive actions and even minor variances create a need to publish a revised plan.

Publishing a revised plan is similar to publishing the original plan during the planning steps of the project management life cycle. If there are any alterations to the resource demands, either in number or time frame, new commitments must be obtained from the managers of those resources. If there is a change in the completion date or the cost at completion, approval of the revised plan may have to be obtained from senior management and the client. Finally, the revised plans have to be distributed to the same persons who were recipients of the original plans.

All status reports and revisions can be published or only exception reports can be produced. Exception reports describe key extracts of the plan, not the entire overview. When you make this decision, consider a form of exception reporting for your own sake (as the person producing the report) as well as the sake of those on your distribution list who have limited time and energy to read your status reports. Following is a list of possible variations of exception reports:

*Schedule*

- Status of tasks on the critical path(s) that have slipped, the reason for their slippage, and the plan to get back on target.
- High-risk tasks for which contingency plans were developed in the planning process. Also, uncertainty paths—those that precede the high-risk tasks—should be tracked. If they slip, then the high-risk tasks are in even more jeopardy.
- Tasks that are eating up their float through slippages.
- Tasks that have extended past their late start or late finish dates.

*Resources*

- Resources not working on committed tasks.
- Resources not possessing the required qualifications.
- Resources working more hours than planned to catch up on schedule slippage.
- Resources working on unapproved changes of scope instead of planned task work.
- Resources being pulled on and off the project erratically.
- Resources not getting along together.
- Resources working a lot of overtime and getting burned out.

*Costs*

- The financial impact of money being thrown into resources.
- Changes in prices or charge-out rates originally used in the plan.

- Additional dollars being spent on new design ideas that were not funded.

## Step 5: Inform Management

During the controlling process, management needs to be informed of problems being experienced on the project so that it can respond to inquiries concerning the project. Management may be asked to provide information or insights necessary to take corrective or preventive action in response to a problem. In addition, management must be given an overall picture of the condition of the project, the problems that have been encountered, and the actions that have been taken in response to the problems.

Management is kept informed through:

- Informal discussions about problems being experienced in the execution of the work and requests for input to the development of solutions.
- Formal presentations (on an infrequent basis) that provide a subjective assessment of the condition of the project.
- Written single-project status reports, prepared each month, that convey a detailed picture of the project.
- Tabular multiproject status reports, giving a very brief summary of the condition of a group of projects.

When deciding whether to distribute status reports to management to keep them informed, remember that people retain only 10 percent of what they read, 20 percent of what they hear, 30 percent of what they see, and 45 percent of what they see and hear (see Figure 7-2). This indicates that a management briefing in which you give a presentation using good graphical representations of the project status, issues, and resolutions is the most effective. Below are some basic guidelines to keep in mind when communicating with management:

- *Objectives:* Continually readdress the project objectives to keep the goal clear in everyone's mind.
- *Simplicity:* Keep communications simple, clear, and concise.
- *Approvals:* Be sure you have obtained appropriate approvals for any changes.
- *Authority levels:* Permit project plans to be changed by authorized people only.
- *Accuracy:* Be sure that everything you display or publish is accurate. This means that all numbers add and cross reference; it also means that reality is portrayed with integrity and honesty.
- *Problem isolation:* Identify project problems primarily through peo-

**Figure 7-2.** Project control: steps to ensure that actual performance conforms to plan.

**Reading**
**10% of what we read**

**Hearing**
**20% of what we hear**

**Seeing**
**30% of what we see**

**Seeing and Hearing**
**45% of what we see and hear**

ple, not paper. Use upward and downward communication techniques.

- *Management by exception:* Establish key indicators. Everything does not have to be communicated; management is interested in just the exceptions.
- *Thresholds:* Establish clear thresholds under which management does not need to be informed and thresholds over which management is to be told about the problem, preferably with recommended solutions.
- *Relevant reports:* Produce only reports useful to management.
- *Review meetings:* Do not use project review meetings as the vehicle for presenting problems to top management for the first time. Inform them beforehand of the issues.

The bottom line is that systems are not a substitute for leadership and effective day-to-day management.

## Project Team Members' Role in the Controlling Process

Consider status information. With respect to completed tasks, the data required include actual task start date, actual task duration, actual person-hours, and actual costs incurred. The first three of these four items should be available from the organization's time reporting system, and the fourth should be available from the cost accounting system. Therefore, it should not be necessary to ask team members for this information, diverting attention from the work at hand.

With respect to tasks that have not yet commenced, the data required include revised duration, revised person-hours required, and revised cost. If the organization has an adequate change management procedure, this information should be available from the current approved plan, which consists of the original project plan plus the approved changes to date. The project team members participated in the development of the estimates for the changes and do not need to be asked about the impact of the change. Furthermore, if a new change to the plan is required, the change management procedure has the team member elevate the need to the attention of the project manager. Therefore, the project manager does not need to ask if there are any revisions to the estimates of future tasks. Once again, the team member may be left to work undisturbed on the project.

The most complex data requirements are those with respect to tasks that are underway at the end of the control period. Data required with respect to these tasks include actual start date, actual days worked, actual person-hours, actual cost, estimated days to complete, estimated person-hours to complete, and estimated cost to complete. Again, there are sources for some of these data other than project team members. Actual start date, actual days worked, and actual person-hours should be available from the time reporting system. Actual cost to date should be available from the cost accounting system. The estimates to complete, however, must come from the project team members; there is simply no other source of these data.

A well-thought-out data collection effort in an organization with adequate time reporting and cost accounting systems can reduce the number of data that have to be gathered from the members of the project team, allowing them more time to work on the project and furthering the objectives of the organization. If the organization's systems are inadequate, the project team members become the primary source of all data. This results in lower productivity and higher estimates for performing the work. Relying on the project team members as the source of data, rather than fixing the time reporting and cost accounting systems, is a poor long-term strategy for the organization.

# Chapter 8

# Project Control Techniques: Status Reports and Reviews

## Designing and Producing Status Report Documents

Do you work in a department or division where everyone who writes a status report uses the same general format? Our guess is that you probably do not. In several informal surveys we have taken, less than 10 percent of project managers within the same organization have a standardized reporting format. How do you as a status reporter know what to report if there are no guidelines? Who teaches you how to construct an informative, concise report with which to keep management abreast of project performance? Typically a status report contains five sections:

### Format for a Status Report

---

Section 1.  Where are we today?
Section 2.  Where will we be at the next report?
Section 3.  What is our budget position?
Section 4.  What items jeopardize project completion?
Section 5.  Who deserves recognition?

---

*Section 1: Where are we today?* This first section gives a brief synopsis of the project's progress since the last status report. You can do this with a list of bulleted items no more than one or two sentences each. Each item describes recent achievements, milestones completed, and other events that have had significant impact on the project (vendor issues, personnel items). Then provide a milestone chart giving a historical perspective of thirty to sixty days. A chart provides a quick context, or background, for the reader to compare planned versus actual performance. This section also provides a high-level project perspective for the purposes of management review. In other words, it keeps the detail level low, provides concise data, pinpoints situations that merit attention, and allows readers the opportunity to request further information as needed. Keep in mind that your audience is inundated with written reports, memos, and other documentation. Your goal is to provide an adequate description of the project, in a short format, that is readable—and will more than likely be read.

*Section 2: Where will we be at the next report?* Once you have brought the reader up to date, describe the project's near-term direction—the events that will take place during the next reporting interval. Again, use one-to-two-sentence bulleted items describing pending events, and prepare a milestone chart with a thirty- to sixty-day forward view. This chart can be combined into a single graphic with the milestone chart from Section 1. Most PC-based project management software packages can easily create this type of chart.

This section gives upper managers a view of the project's immediate direction. In this way, they have the opportunity to suggest course corrections early enough to make an impact on project progress.

*Section 3: What is our budget position?* It is very important that this section be a clear visual image. Detailed charts with mounds of data and dozens of line items get ignored unless a project is in serious trouble. Prepare a simple line graph or a bar chart that displays plan versus actual data. If there is significant variance in actual versus plan, provide a brief explanation of the cause of the variance. This simple chart gives managers enough basic data to assess overall project budgetary status. If they want more detail, they will request it.

*Section 4: What items jeopardize project completion?* HELP! That's really what this section is about. Let management know where there is a problem and what should be done about it. There are two criteria for an item to be included in this section: It must place the completion of the project at risk, and it must be beyond your capability to resolve. If both these conditions are met, ask for help in clear tones. (If not, resolve the issue yourself and go on). Be sure you indicate clearly what action you would like management to take. This is not an opportunity to take a monkey off your back and put it onto your boss's. It's your chance to call in the cavalry. But you need to be explicit in describing the help you need.

A political side note is required here: Inform your manager of any items you intend to include in this section before you print the report. Managers do not like to be caught unaware, and it is a politically adroit project manager who gives a manager a chance to resolve problems before they reach print.

*Section 5: Who deserves recognition?* This last section is very important and often overlooked. Team members, not just project managers, make or break a project. Their involvement, commitment, and dedication to quality make the difference between success and failure. Yet we often overlook basic opportunities to recognize team members who demonstrate excellence on the job, put in long days and weekends, forsake vacations and holidays, and walk that extra mile to make a project successful. This section allows you to acknowledge excellence and dedication. As a morale boost, it demonstrates to the project team that you are aware of the work being done and are appreciative. It also provides visibility for the productive workers to upper management.

Adapt these five sections to your own situation in order to improve communication with management. Encourage your peers to adopt a format they will all employ. You will find that a short, concise status report is a management tool, not drudgery. Managers will learn what to expect in a status report and where to find it. The key to a status report is how effectively it communicates the state of the project to management, but it has to be read first. Make it concise.

### Charts and Graphs

There are a variety of graphic presentations that can effectively compare planned versus actual performance. Remember that status reports give us the questions. You not only need to address these questions but also find solutions and implement action plans.

The typical Gantt chart shown in Figure 8-1 indicates that Activities 3, 5, and 6 have started later than planned. Some of the questions you need to be asking are the following: Are these slippages on the critical path? If they are, is there a way to make up the lost time? If these slippages are on noncritical activities, has the slippage eaten up all the available float? What caused the slippage?

The Gantt chart in Figure 8-2 shows a dramatic slippage on all activities. Among the questions you need to ask are these: Why did the project start late? Why did Activity A take twice as long to complete? Critical path Activity E has started one and a half months late. Is there any chance of completing this activity on time? (Probably not.) Most important, why are we living with this unrealistic schedule? Where is the revised plan?

Now let's look at Figure 8-3. This Gantt chart shows an early completion of critical path Activity E. However, noncritical path Activity C has slipped one month. As you can see, the noncritical path Activity F has one and a half months of float, which can accommodate the slippage in C. With the early completion of E, however, the C,F path has now become the critical path.

Here are some questions that you should ask: What is taking so long in Activity C? If it completes within the next half-month, we have a

*(Text continues on page 138.)*

**Figure 8-1.** Typical Gantt chart.

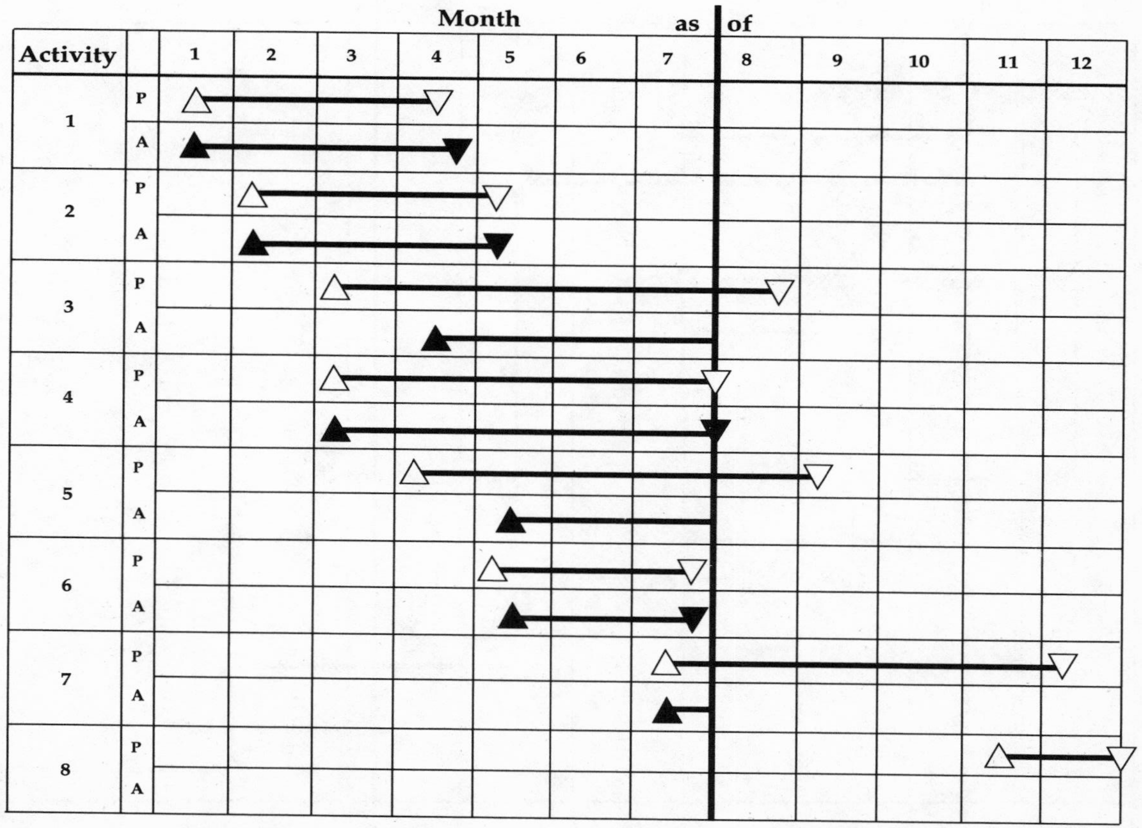

P = planned date.
A = actual date.

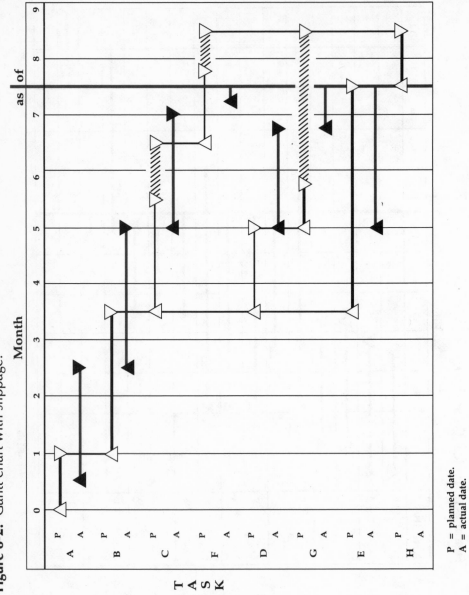

**Figure 8-2.** Gantt chart with slippage.

P = planned date.
A = actual date.

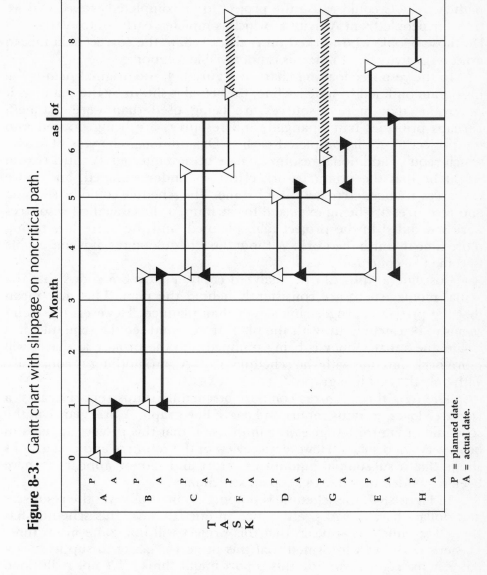

**Figure 8-3.** Gantt chart with slippage on noncritical path.

P = planned date.
A = actual date.

chance of completing the project early. If not, the initially noncritical path Activity C could cause the project to be completed late. Could we transfer people from Activity E, which completed early, onto Activity C? Do those people who worked on Activity E have the correct skill mix to work on Activity C? If not, this is not a viable solution.

In the resource loading chart in Figure 8-4, the original plan is the histogram outlined by a heavy line; the actual is shown by the shading. It is obvious that more resources are being used than were planned. Perhaps priorities have changed, and resources are being poured into the project to get it completed earlier. Or additional changes of scope, which require additional resources, have been requested. A third reason might be that the original work effort ws underestimated, and more resources are needed to get the job done. The schedule could be slipping and resources are being expected to catch up, or less qualified resources were scheduled to the project than planned, and therefore it is taking more time to finish the work. Without the schedule status, it is impossible to come to a conclusion.

Cost line graphs can be analyzed easily. Figure 8-5 shows that the actual monies spent are consistently behind the plan. This may mean that the project is progressing slower than planned. However, the trend seems to be catching up with the plan. If we could see the schedule, it is a safe guess that money is being pumped into the project so that it will move back into line with the schedule plan. Again, nothing is conclusive with only the cost line graph.

The next three figures compare a schedule status report against a resource loading status report and a cost line graph. A first glance at the schedule in Figure 8-6 gives the impression that this project appears to be in very good shape. However, a review of the resource and cost graphs shows that a substantial amount of effort and money appears to have been expended in order to keep on schedule.

In Figure 8-7, the schedule is slipping dramatically, yet the resources and dollars have stayed pretty much in line. Because this schedule has slipped so much, it appears that this project will not come in on time. Has everyone been informed that this project is going to slip its target date? A manager reviewing this report might think, "It's not realistic to expect that the resources will start dropping off, or the budget. Looks like we should be negotiating to keep some of the resources on the project in order to make up for lost time. We'll also want to project an overbudget position at completion—and we may want to cancel the project if the benefits planned will not be accomplished."

In Figure 8-8, the schedule is slipping too. Completion dates for work activities have been extended, probably because the resources planned for the project have not been available. The underbudget situation is not necessarily good news, since the projections seem to indicate a final late completion and overbudget situation.

*(Text continues on page 144.)*

**Figure 8-4.** Resource loading chart.

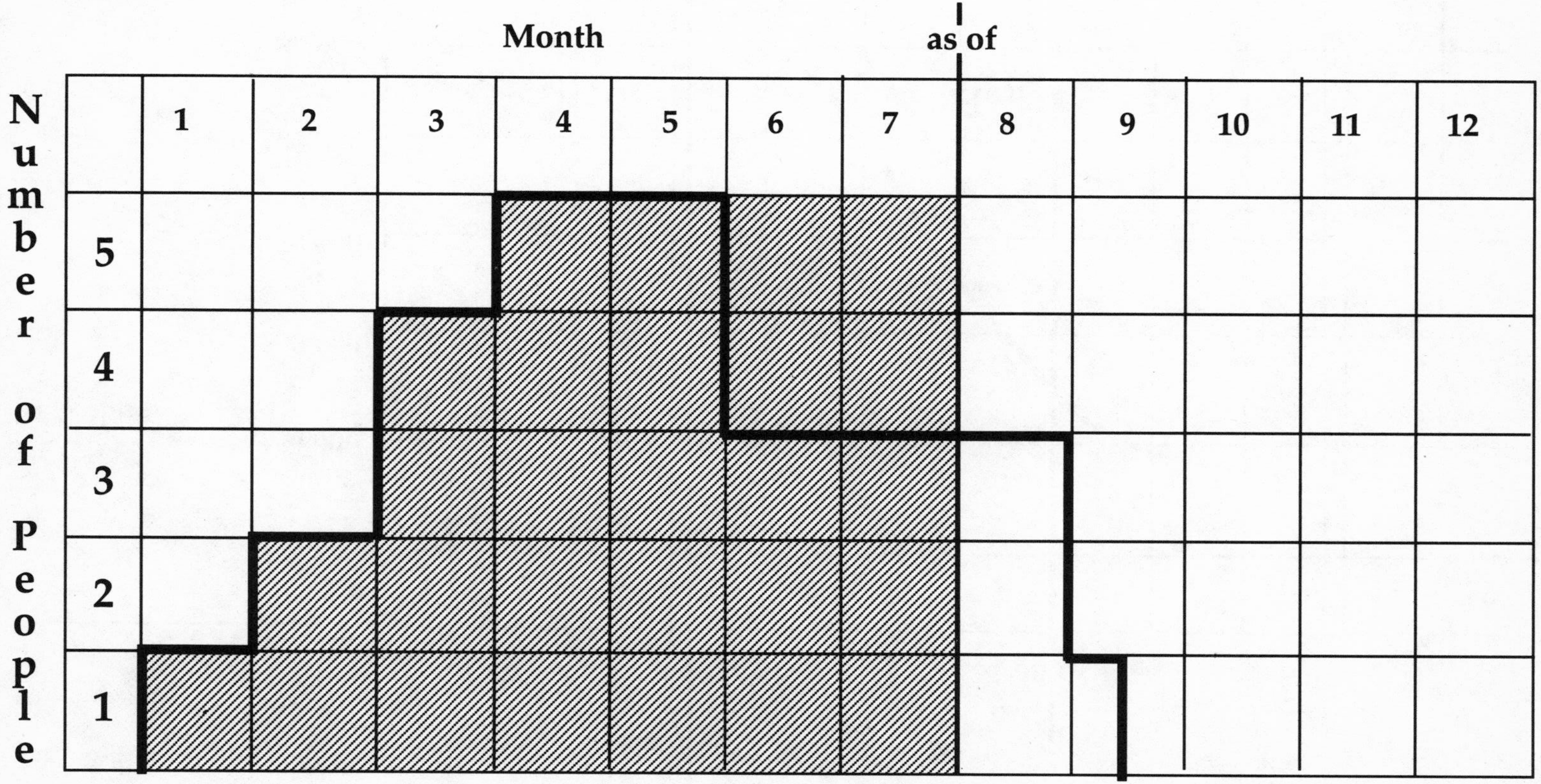

**Figure 8-5.** Cost line graph.

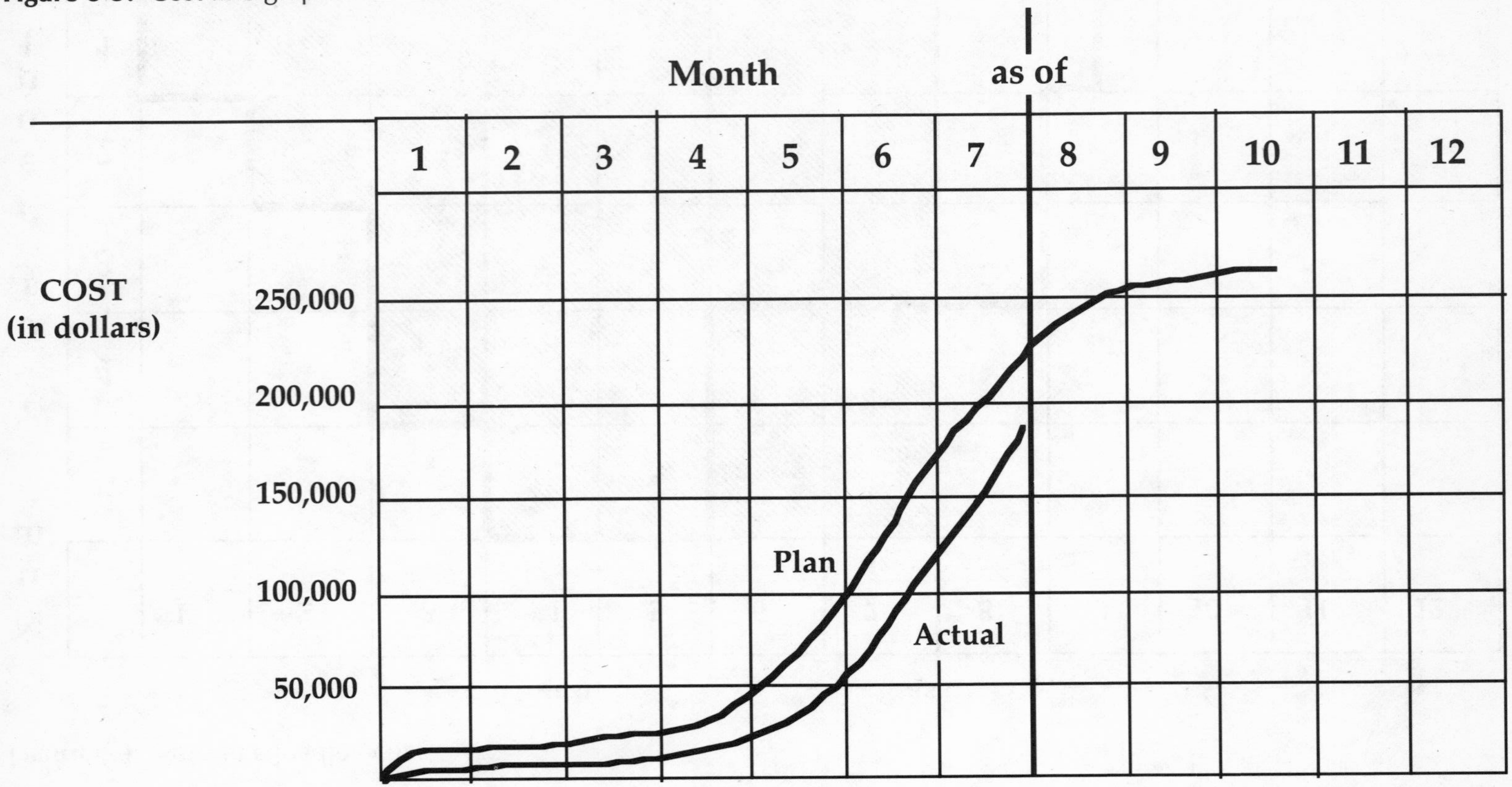

**Figure 8-6.** Multiple baselines.

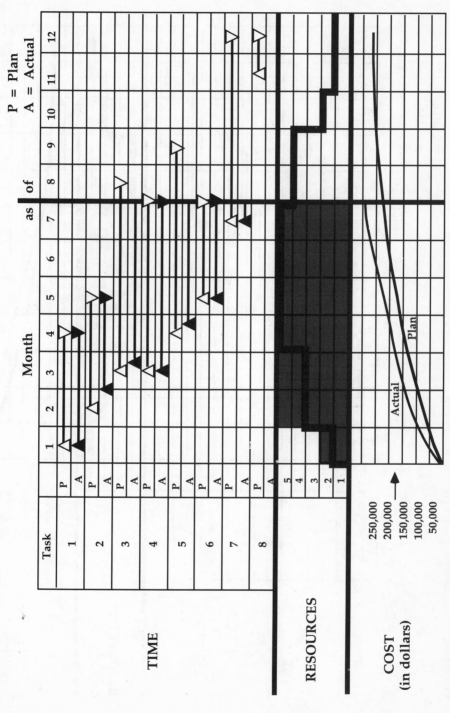

**Figure 8-7.** Multiple baselines with slippage.

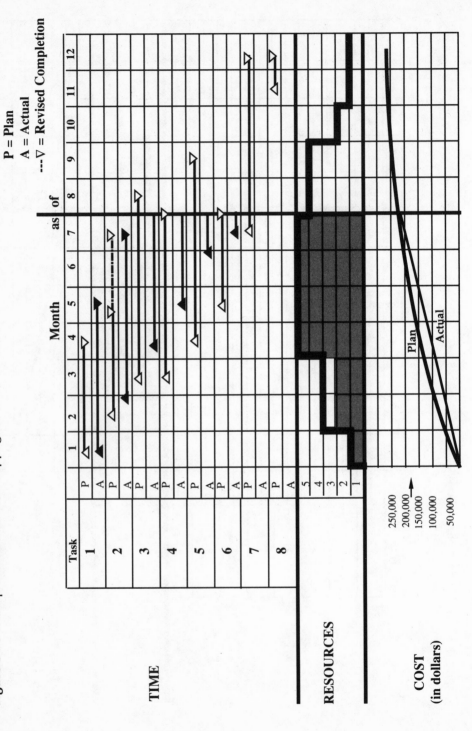

**Figure 8-8.** Multiple baselines with slippage and underbudget situation.

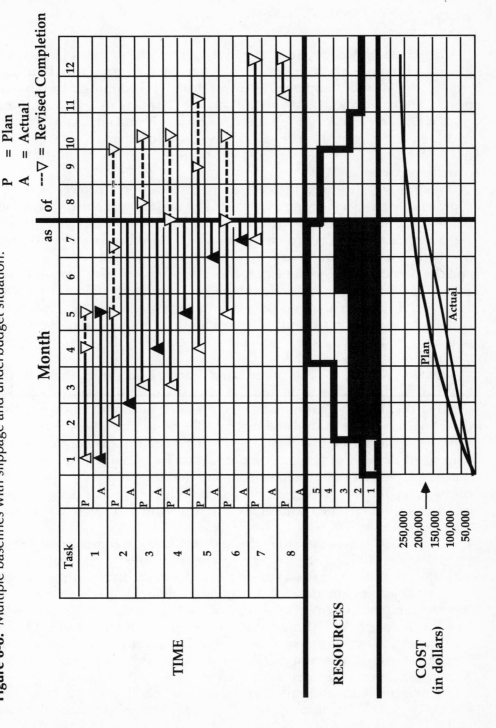

### *Trend Analysis*

In the preceding section, we analyzed snapshots of a project at a moment in time. However, there is more to reporting project status than just telling people what happened as of yesterday. It is important to look at trends and to project what will ultimately happen in terms of time, resources, and/or dollars if the trend continues. Trend analysis is a useful tool for project control since it enables you to compare the target with the destination. Let's compare two illustrations in order to illustrate the benefits of trend analysis.

Figure 8-9 illustrates the cost analysis curve for a project as of the completion of a specific control period. The target represents the current plan—what the project manager is aiming for in terms of schedule and cost. The destination represents the current forecast for schedule and cost completion. There is usually some discrepancy between the target and the destination. The same graph can be produced with person-hours as its y-axis; in this case, the destination represents the current forecast for schedule completion and person-hours at completion. The problem is that the destination changes from month to month, and the graph does not allow the project manager to perceive the change in the destination.

Trend analysis, on the other hand, focuses on the changes in the destination. It allows you to see the changes over time and to decide whether the trend is alarming, though the current forecast indicates that the project will be completed within the plan plus the contingency allocated to it. In Figure 8-10, the most recent forecasted completion date, as of the end of the sixth month, is twelve and a half months, but the trend indicates fourteen and a half months. Since the plan plus contingency for the project is fourteen months, it looks as if the project may be in trouble. The trend analysis has provided an early warning of the problem.

Figure 8-11 indicates that the trended cost at completion will be $25,000 over budget. Since the graph indicates a contingency of $100,000, the cost does not appear to be a problem. In fact, the manager of this project might do well to spend additional funds in order to shorten the period of performance, if possible. Similarly, the resource trend in Figure 8-12 indicates that the ceiling on human resources for the project will not be approached, given the current trend. Just over 40 percent of the reserves are forecasted to be utilized by the trended completion date of fourteen and a half months.

The trend in the utilization of contingency can also be tracked. Here a word of warning is appropriate: Tracking contingency utilization requires a good deal of planning. First, the risks must be identified. Then the time frame for each risk must be anticipated. Figure 8-13 presents a sample of such a trend analysis. In this example, contingency utilization

*(Text continues on page 150.)*

**Figure 8-9.** Cost analysis curve.

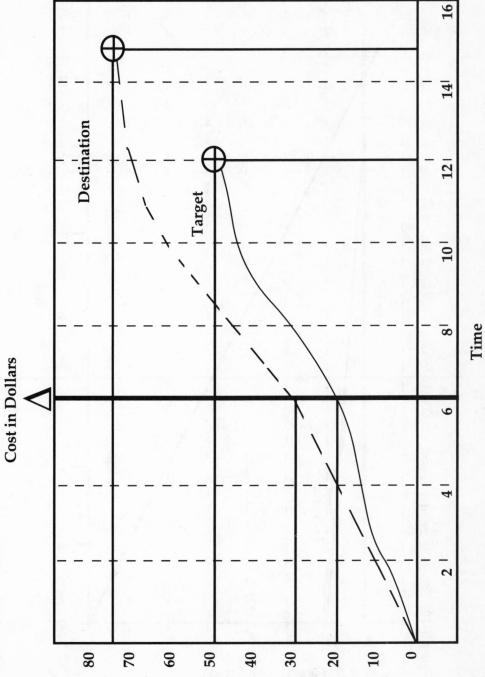

**Figure 8-10.** Schedule trend analysis.

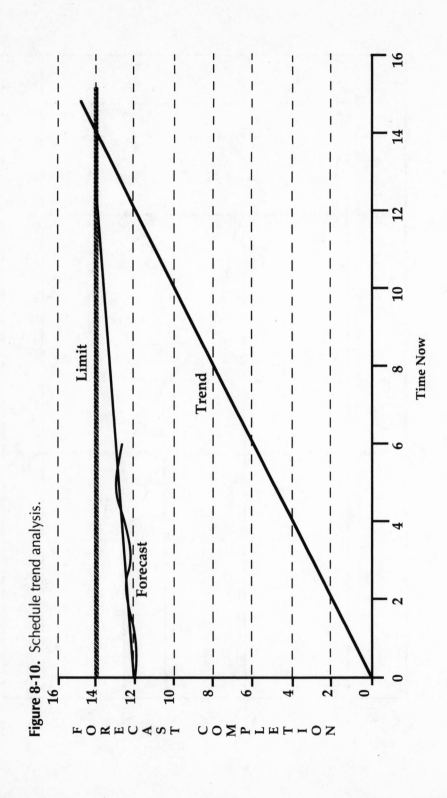

**Figure 8-11.** Cost trend.

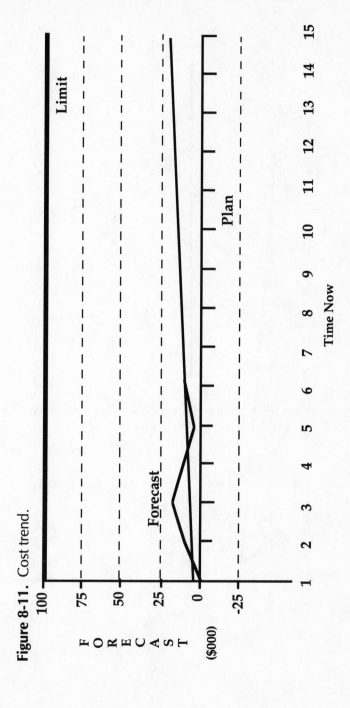

**Figure 8-12.** Resource trend analysis.

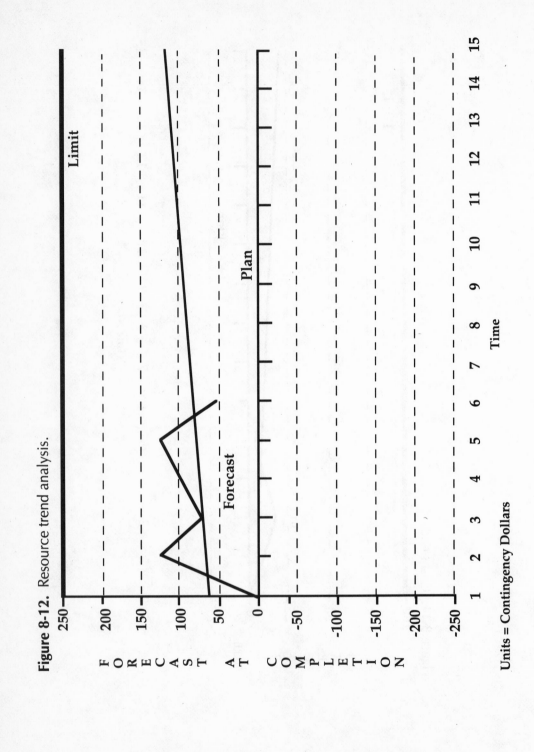

Units = Contingency Dollars

**Figure 8-13.** Contingency utilization.

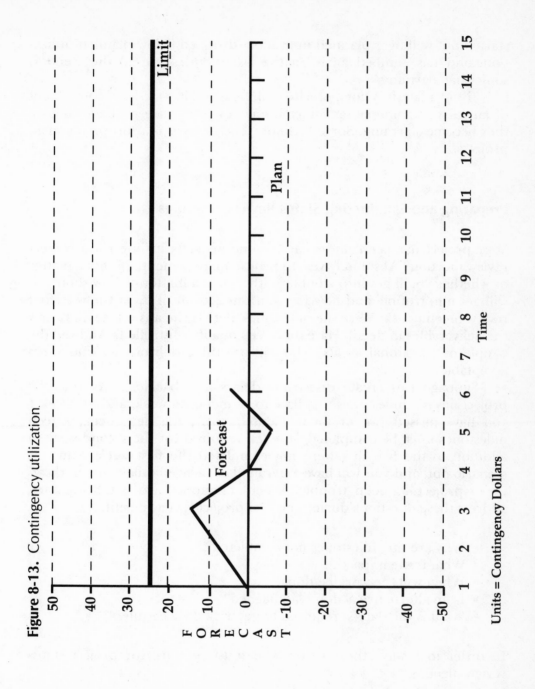

Units = Contingency Dollars

started out well over planned utilization, dropped below planned utilization, and has climbed again in the last month. Overall the trend is somewhat alarming.

Trend analysis is not a precise tool; however, it is a critical component of an early warning system since it enables you to see problems before they become alarming. Some form of trend analysis is appropriate on all projects.

## Preparing and Conducting Status Review Meetings

Your project has been underway for one week. Is it time for a project review meeting? Absolutely yes. In project management, it is not a matter of whether you'll get into trouble; rather, it is a matter of how soon you will get into trouble and how fast you can get out of it. At the very first review meeting ask: Were the milestones met? If the answer is yes, review the deliverables in detail. Have they been quality controlled? And will the people or functional area(s) who will use these deliverables find them acceptable?

Slippage can create disastrous delays and backlogs. Assume the project has ten milestones that have to be met each week, and on Week 1 you have missed five of them. Consequently, the next week, fifteen milestones must be completed—the ten required for the second week in addition to the five that were not completed the first week. Run this scenario out, and you will have a pyramid of delayed milestones, indicating a project in deep trouble. When milestones are not being met, address these questions during the first project review meeting:

- Why are the milestones not completed?
- What is the impact?
- When will the work be done?
- Is an alternative action plan needed?
- What is the date(s) required to get back on schedule?

In order to resolve these issues, you must prepare for project status review meetings.

### How to Prepare for a Review Meeting

- *Define the objective of the meeting clearly.* Each project review meeting cannot cover in detail all of the project issues—the schedule, budget, resource utilization, quality, technical, and design considerations. Therefore, the objective should be focused and determined by the participants.

For example, if the attendees are the management committee and/or the customer, they will want to know about what has gone wrong, what you have done to fix it, and what, if any, support you need from them. If the audience is the project team, you will be concerned about the fundamental nitty-gritty areas. You and the team want to know about what has been done, what slipped, what impact the slippage had, what you will do about it, and what is coming up in the near future. With these issues in perspective, you have the basis for a renewed commitment to completion.

▪ *Prepare a well-thought-out agenda.* Allocate your agenda time wisely. Cover the most important topics early when people are alert and will address them with vigor. On your copy of the agenda, insert the scheduled time for each topic in the margin. Allow some buffer time should the topic take longer than expected. Preview the agenda with the appropriate people to ensure that you have not omitted anything, included anything that is extraneous, or neglected to clarify the objective of each topic.

▪ *Invite the essential people.* It serves no purpose to have all concerned parties attend each meeting. There is a core team that should be present, but beyond that, the balance of the team members should be encouraged to attend only when they have something to contribute or have a need to be kept informed. A project review meeting on the first Monday of every month could become tedious should the agenda have no relevance to the current activities of the attendees.

▪ *Dry run your speakers.* You as project manager should not always make the entire presentation. For example, an engineer may report on a technical design, a marketing representative on a sales strategy, or a computer programmer on a new automated system. Before the presentation, request your speakers to walk through (talk through) their presentation, for both their benefit and yours. It is too late to make modifications when they are in front of the audience and presenting erroneous or inappropriate data.

▪ *Organize the project review meeting to your best advantage.* As the first speaker, you need to present briefly and concisely an overview of the meeting, the objective of it, and a quick preview of the agenda. With this effective form of introduction, you set the tone and alert the participants to your major concerns.

### How to Conduct a Review Meeting

▪ *Follow the agenda.* Once the agenda is set, follow it. Do not stray from the format. If an attendee attempts to circumvent your game plan, use the agenda to bring the subject back into focus. Typically your agenda should cover the following subjects:

### Typical Agenda for a Project Review Meeting

- Major accomplishments since the last review.
- Schedule status (actual versus plan).
- Financial status (actual versus plan, including a clear explanation of variances from plan).
- Major issues (problems) and action plans. Indicate specific assistance required from management or the customer, as well as from any of the functional areas within the matrix (action plans should include a deliverable(s) and deadlines).
- Plans for the next period.
- Special topics (those with a sense of urgency).
- Review of action items generated from this meeting and a time and place for the next meeting.

A number of questions will help you gain the information you need:

### Suggested Questions for a Project Review Meeting

- Do you foresee any future problems?
- Is your personnel supply in jeopardy? Are people being pulled off projects?
- Is there dissatisfaction among your staff? What's bothering them?
- How are you dealing with recurrent problems?
- What are you lacking to do your job?
- Have you prepared for long lead deliveries?
- Are you accepting substantive changes that should be addressed in a change control (change of scope) process?

- *Don't overrun your agenda.* Most attendees' schedules are tight; therefore, they will probably allocate just so much time to your review meeting. There is a prevailing feeling that too much time is spent in meetings, so make the briefing concise and stay on target. Record time allotment on the margin of your working agenda. Maintain your pace, and move on when you need to. When appropriate, carry over the discussion to the next meeting. Assign team members the responsibility for investigating subjects and reviewing the results in advance of the next meeting. Remember the rule of thumb: People can be productive in a meeting environment for approximately one to one and a half hours. After that, it's all downhill.

Remember that a well-run review meeting is the forum in which to accomplish many of your key objectives as project manager: to improve communication, motivate the project team, maintain control, evaluate status, isolate problems, and institute action plans. Use this opportunity well.

### Senior Management Reviews

Project management reports are generated for senior management on a recurring basis, usually at the end of each cyclical reporting period. These reports, in conjunction with review meetings, afford you a wonderful opportunity to interact with senior management. In order to maximize this opportunity, make sure that your project reports for senior management review meetings take less than thirty minutes. The review of the project status should be structured according to five topics:

1. *Project introduction:* Summarize the project objectives and the composition of the project team.
2. *Problems:* Present each problem being faced by the team and include the worst-case scenario, the action required to fix the problem, and the approvals required to implement the solution.
3. *Subjective appraisal:* Give your assessment of the state of the project and the degree of client satisfaction with the effort.
4. *Outstanding decisions:* Enumerate the decision that senior management and the client must make, as well as the consequences of a delay in receiving the decisions.
5. *Status:* Present summary project-management-system displays of the schedule, cost, resource, and accomplishment states of the project.

# Chapter 9

# A Model for Earned Value: Achievement-Accomplishment Monitoring

In this chapter, we explore how to assess the state of the project based on milestone completions—what is often called *earned value* or *achievement-accomplishment monitoring*. Achievement monitors the completion of milestones. Accomplishment assesses earned value. Earned value shows how much work has been accomplished and can be used to determine performance standards and to forecast mathematically time and/or dollars needed to complete the project. It can provide much more information than just whether the project is ahead of or behind schedule, over or under budget, and/or being efficient or inefficient with the organization's money.

Achievement and accomplishment serve the same purpose. They allow you to draw conclusions concerning the accuracy of the estimates-to-complete furnished by the members of the project team. But the quality of the information is not the same. Achievement monitoring is an intuitive, judgmental process in which you and the team members infer the project status from the unique trends and dynamics produced over the project's life cycle. Accomplishment planning and control allows a quantified comparison with person-hour and dollar expenditures, as well as schedule status.

Both approaches are based on milestones, which are identified during the development of the project plan, and each works best if there are a significant number of milestones, with at least a few scheduled to be completed during each progress-monitoring period.

## The Role of Milestones

A *milestone* is a marker for a major event—a significant point in development. In the world of information systems, a milestone might be the delivery of an internal design or systems test. In construction, a milestone might be the delivery of materials. And in research and development, funding or completion of a prototype test might be considered a milestone.

Before that milestone can ever be met, a series of smaller markers must be passed. Waiting to check progress until a major milestone is reached is an invitation to disaster. It is these small deliverables that you will be managing. What is due today? If it isn't ready, when will it be? What is needed to get back on track?

In achievement monitoring, milestones are not weighted on the basis of complexity or difficulty. They are identified and incorporated into the project schedule. A milestone schedule is developed so that you know when each milestone is scheduled to be achieved. During the course of informal project control or management by wandering around, you must verify the timely completion of the milestones and indicate their completion on the project status report. Finally, you must use the achievement data to assess whether the cost and schedule estimates are consistent with the achievement to date. Consistent data should raise your level of confidence; inconsistent data will raise doubts about the estimates-to-complete furnished by task leaders.

In performing an assessment of achievement to date, it is not possible to determine the worth of the completed milestones as a percentage of the total worth of the project milestones. An invalid conclusion would be to infer that 33 percent of a project has been achieved because twenty-five of seventy-five milestones are completed. It may be interesting to know that twenty-five of seventy-five milestones have been completed, but the project might be only 5 percent complete—or 95 percent complete—based on the relative worth of those milestones.

Accomplishment monitoring contains several added steps. The first step is the same: Identify the milestones and incorporate them into the project schedule. The second step, developing a milestone schedule, is also the same regardless of whether achievement or accomplishment is being used. But the third step is complex. Each milestone must be given a difficulty weight, which forms the basis of the earned value calculations and the mathematical assessment of the yield of efforts to date (a subject discussed later in this chapter). During the course of informal project control or management by wandering around, verify the timely completion of the milestones and indicate their completion on the project status report. Finally, make the earned value calculations and use them to check the consistency of the earned value data with the cost and schedule estimates. Consistency can raise your level of confidence; inconsistency can raise doubts about the estimates-to-complete furnished by the task leaders.

The critical issue in accomplishment monitoring is to determine how milestones are weighted. The Department of Defense (and other government agencies that use milestone reporting) prefers to use the milestone budget as an indicator of the worth of the milestone. Thus, the percentage of completion of the project is calculated by dividing the budget of the completed milestones by the total direct cost budget of the project. If $5,650 worth of milestones have been completed out of a total budget of $25,000, the project is said to be 22.6 percent complete. The major problem in using budget as the weight for the milestones is the purchased item distortion. Purchased items that are not difficult to obtain but are high-cost items receive a disproportionately high value in the calculation of percentage complete.

Other organizations use person-hours, labor budgets, or expert assigned points. In the person-hour approach, the percentage of completion of the project is calculated by dividing the planned person-hours of the completed milestones by the total person-hours of the project. While this eliminates the purchased item distortion, it creates its own distortion in which tasks requiring a large number of hours of unskilled labor are valued more highly than tasks requiring slightly fewer hours of the most skilled professionals in the organization.

In the labor budget approach, the percentage of completion of the project is calculated by dividing the labor budget of the completed milestones by the total labor budget of the project. This reduces the distortion created by tasks requiring large amounts of unskilled labor, but it is based on an assumption that may not prove true: that people are compensated on the basis of the value of their contribution to the effort.

Using a group of experts to assign point values to each of the project milestones yields the most accurate results. In this approach, the percentage of completion of the project is calculated by dividing the point values of the completed milestones by the total point values of all project milestones. This approach is the least frequently used, however, since the added cost of assigning points to the milestones, and revising the point values if the project scope changes, can be great.

Any of these weighting techniques can be used at the end of a period in order to derive a planned percentage of completion for the project and an actual percentage of completion for comparison purposes. The data can be further analyzed as checks on the status being reported by the members of the project team.

Because many project control techniques do not focus on the physical completion of work or do not place sufficient emphasis on this factor, either achievement or accomplishment monitoring needs to be part of every organization's approach to project management. Many organizations ought to consider developing a procedure for each approach so they can apply the achievement approach to smaller, less significant projects and the accomplishment approach to larger, more visible, and more critical projects.

## Achievement Monitoring

Achievement monitoring works best when there are many milestones in the plan. The example in Figure 9-1 uses a milestone plan for a ten-month project. Each box with a number inside represents a milestone. The number equals the budget dollars for each milestone. Zeros have been eliminated.

Let's examine the potential achievement status of the project at the end of the fifth month. If we monitor cost and schedule performance, then we will expect the project to be 50 percent complete (five months of a ten-month project completed). If completion of milestones is the measuring criterion, then at the end of five months, we could expect the project to be 48 percent complete (ten of twenty-one milestones completed). We can also expect that 70 budget dollars (sum of milestone budgets for the first five months) out of a total of 126 budget dollars (sum for all milestones) will have been completed, or 55 percent complete (70/126). Thus we have a range of expectations from 48 percent complete to 55 percent complete, with the 55 percent completion clearly being accurate because it is based on earned value.

Figure 9-2 presents the actual milestone completions at the end of the fifth month. Note that Milestone 8 has been completed ahead of schedule, while Milestone 13 should have been completed over a month ago. The value of the completed milestones is 65 (the sum of the completed milestones budgets). Using earned value, the project is actually 51.5 percent complete (65/126). The project is 3.5 percent behind where it ought to be (55 percent − 51.5 percent).

Now let us assume that the cost accounting system tells us that we spent \$73 to complete the current milestones (this is an arbitrary number we have chosen for the sake of the example). This information will enable us to anticipate the information to be generated by the members of the project team and will thereby demonstrate the power of earned value. We can expect the members of the project team to report that they are behind schedule by approximately 7.1 percent. The difference between the budgets of the planned milestones (70) and the completed milestones (65), divided by the budget of the planned milestones [(70 − 65)/70] gives this result. However, we can expect the members of the project team to report that they are under budget by approximately 12.3 percent. The difference between the budgets of the completed milestones (65) and the cost incurred to complete them (73), divided by the budget of the completed milestones [(65 − 73)/65] gives this result.

## Analysis of Accomplishment Data

The effort that goes into calculating the weighted value of completed milestones can yield information useful to you over and above the ability

**Figure 9-1.** Milestone plan for a ten-month project. Each numbered box is a milestone; the number in each box shows the budget dollars for it.

| Phase | Jan | Feb | Mar | Apr | May | June | July | Aug | Sept | Oct | Nov | Dec |
|---|---|---|---|---|---|---|---|---|---|---|---|---|
| A | 5 | 4 | | | | | | | | | | |
| B | | 6 7 | 5 | | | | | | | | | |
| C | | | 8 3 | 9 | | | | | | | | |
| D | | | | | 10 | | | | | | | |
| E | | | | | | | 8 | | | | | |
| F | | | | | | | 2 | 11 | | | | |
| G | | | | 13 | | | | | | | | |
| H | | | | | | | | 6 | 3 4 | | | |
| I | | | | | | | | | 2 | 3 | | |
| J | | | | | | | | | 5 | 5 | | |
| K | | | | | | | | | | 7 | | |

to report accurately a percentage of completion at the close of a reporting period. The analyses we will use here can be performed with any rational weighting scheme for milestones—budget, labor budget, person-hours, or expert assigned points. For this discussion, we will assume that milestones have been weighted on the basis of their budgets.

### Comparison of Budgeted Cost of Milestones Scheduled and Budgeted Cost of Milestones Performed

A comparison of the budgeted cost of milestones scheduled (BCMS) and the budgeted cost of milestones performed (BCMP) yields an assessment of schedule performance on the project:

#### Three Typical Interpretations for Schedule Performance

1. If BCMS is greater than BCMP, the project is behind schedule.
2. If these two values are equal, the project is on schedule.
3. If the BCMP is greater than BCMS, the project is ahead of schedule.

These values are calculated from your verification of milestone completions rather than by reports from the task leaders. If task leaders report milestone completions, these analyses will not function as a check and balance on cost and schedule progress reporting. When you compare BCMS and BCMP, the results should be consistent with the schedule status as reported by the task leaders through the schedule of estimates-to-complete. If the results are consistent, it is likely that the task leaders' assessment of schedule performance is accurate. If the results are inconsistent, it is likely that there is a problem with the schedule estimates-to-complete rendered by the task leaders.

### Comparison of Budgeted Cost of Milestones Performed and Actual Cost of Milestones Performed

A comparison of the budgeted cost of milestones performed (BCMP) and actual cost of milestones performed (ACMP) yields three assessments of cost performance on the project:

#### Assessments of Cost Performance

1. If BCMP is greater than ACMP, the project is under budget.
2. If these two values are equal, the project is on budget.
3. If the ACMP is greater than BCMP, the project is over budget.

**Figure 9-2.** Actual milestone completions at the end of the project's fifth month.

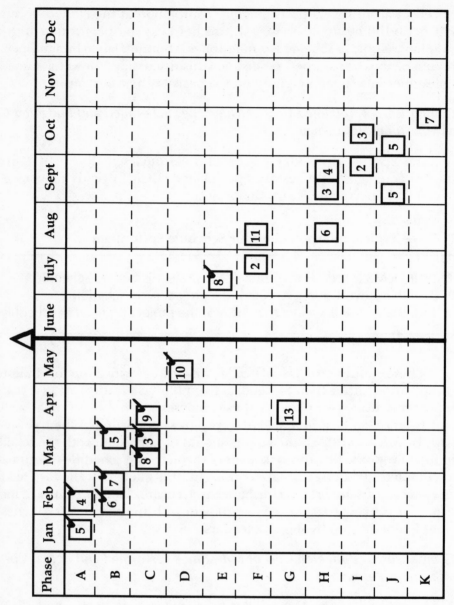

When you compare BCMP and ACMP, the results should be consistent with the cost status reported by the task leaders through the cost estimates-to-complete. If the results are consistent, it is likely that the task leaders' assessment of cost performance is accurate. If they are inconsistent, it is likely that there is a problem with the cost estimates-to-complete rendered by the task leaders.

The problem with cost estimates could stem from an erroneous assessment of cost to complete, it could be unwarranted optimism on the part of the task leaders, or it could be an error in the processing of the data. In any case, you need to determine why there is an inconsistency between cost performance to date and the cost estimates-to-complete.

### Schedule Performance Index and Cost Performance Index

The final element of the analysis is the calculation of two important trends: the schedule performance index (SPI) and the cost performance index (CPI):

#### Key Accomplishment Trends

---

1. The schedule performance index is equal to the budgeted cost of milestones performed divided by the budgeted cost of milestones scheduled.
2. The cost performance index is equal to the budgeted cost of milestones performed divided by the actual cost of milestones performed.

---

Calculate the performance index SPI and CPI at the end of each reporting period. Ideally, each index should be equal to 1, which indicates that actual performance and planned performance are the same. An index value less than 1 indicates you are behind schedule or over budget, and an index value greater than 1 indicates you are ahead of schedule or under budget. Index values calculated at the end of a period of performance add little to the value of the information already available to you. They become meaningful and useful when they are available for a number of periods and can be used to indicate a trend in schedule and/ or cost performance. Plotting these values on a single graph where the x-axis is the end period and the y-axis is the index value will show a clear picture of both the schedule and cost performance trends on the project. You can then see if the index values are changing in an alarming manner or if the change indicates that the project is under control.

## Calculations Using Accomplishment Data

The calculations employed in the analysis of accomplishment data use these acronyms:

BAC    = budget at completion
BCMS = budgeted cost of milestones scheduled (or the planned earned value)
BCMP = budgeted cost of milestones performed (or actual earned value)
ACMP = actual cost of milestones performed (or actual dollars spent)

### Example 1

Activity ABC is to produce 100 units and is scheduled to take 5 weeks. Each unit is planned to cost $75.* Below are the basic data needed to work through this example.

1. *Planned status at the end of the third week.* If 100 units are scheduled to be produced in 5 weeks, 20 units are scheduled to be generated per week if we assume linear production. Therefore, at the end of the third week, 60 units are planned to be produced. If the standard cost of each unit is $75, the BCMS is $4,500.
2. *Actual status at the end of the third week.* Fifty units have been produced, earning the value of $3,750. In other words, 50 units × $75 (standard cost) = $3,750. Therefore, the BCMP is $3,750.
3. *Monies actually spent:* The financial reports indicate that $3,000 has been spent; therefore, the ACMP is $3,000.

To summarize:

- BAC of the project is planned to be $7,500.
- At the end of the third week, BCMS is $4,500, BCMP is $3,750, and ACMP is $3,000.

### Questions:

Here are seven questions that can be answered with the data provided. Work through the calculations; then look up the answers and explanations that follow.

*For purposes of this example, it does not matter whether the units are widgets or miles of pipe or drawings. It is important, however, that a quantifiable measurement of the number of units can be attached to the output from this activity.

1. Project's cost variance = BCMP − ACMP.
   Answer: $_____

   Are we over budget or under budget? _____

2. Schedule variance in cost terms = BCMP − BCMS.
   Answer: $_____

   Are we ahead of or behind schedule? _____

3. Cost performance index (CPI) = BCMP/ACMP.
   Answer: _____

   Are we performing better or worse than planned? _____

4. Schedule performance index (SPI) = BCMP/BCMS.
   Answer: _____

   Are we performing better or worse than planned? _____

5. Budgeted cost for the remaining milestones (BCRM) = BAC − BCMP
   Answer: $_____

6. Estimate to complete the project (ETC) = (BAC − BCMP)/CPI
   Answer: $_____

7. Total estimate at completion (EAC) = ACMP + ETC
   Answer: $_____

### Answers

1. Project's cost variance = BCMP − ACMP. $3,750 − $3,000 = $750 (compares what was planned to be spent against what was actually spent).

   If the answer is a positive figure, less money is being spent than was planned; the project is under budget.
2. Schedule variance in cost terms = BCMP − BCMS. $3,750 − $4,500 = − $750 (compares what was spent in terms of accomplishment as compared to what was planned to be spent).

   If the answer is a negative figure, less work is being accomplished than planned, and the project is behind schedule.
3. Cost performance index (CPI) = BCMP/ACMP. $3,750/$3,000 = 125 percent (compares the ratio of what was accomplished in dollar terms to that which was actually spent).

   If the answer is more than 100 percent, the project performance relative to cost performance is good.
4. Schedule performance index (SPI) = BCMP/BCMS. $3,750/$4,500 = 83.3 percent (compares the ratio of what was accomplished in dollar terms to what was planned to be accomplished).

If the answer is less than 100 percent the project relative to schedule performance is poor.

There is good news and bad news so far. This activity is behind schedule, but the project's money is being spent effectively. In other words, the cost performance is good; more units of work are being accomplished for fewer dollars than planned. The schedule performance is not measuring up to plan, however.

5. Budgeted cost for the remaining milestones (BCRM) = BAC − BCMP. $7,500 − $3,750 = $3,750 (subtracts the accomplishment in dollar terms from the original planned budget at completion).
   This answer indicates how much money is left in the budget.
6. Estimate to complete the project (ETC) = (BAC − BCMP)/CPI. ($7,500 − $3,750)/1.25 = $3,000 (uses the BCRM calculated in Step 5 and takes into account the cost performance index).
   This answer shows the additional money needed to complete the job.
7. Total estimate at completion (EAC) = ACMP + ETC. $3,000 + $3,000 = $6,000 (adds what has already been spent to what yet needs to be spent in order to finish the job).
   This answer anticipates the total budget at the end of the project.

This is only the beginning of the calculations that can be used in accomplishment analysis. The example assumes that Task ABC is accomplished in a linear fashion and that each of the deliverables will be produced at equal intervals and for equal dollars. This may not be true. In fact, much work is accomplished in a nonlinear way.

Often progress is measured over time on the basis of an assumed linear relationship, perhaps because linear extrapolations are easier to calculate than nonlinear ones. But we think that the problem is more complex. In essence, there seems to be a natural tendency to think in terms of linear relationships. When this is coupled with the fact that we live in a nonlinear world, it leads to false assessments of progress and, in turn, diversion of management attention from real problems to apparent problems. This result can be a disaster, even crippling an organization.

As an example, assume that a technician faced with the task of upgrading sixty personal computers can complete the job in sixty hours (this is the technician's estimate). Furthermore, assume that four machines can be completed at the end of the first day. When we examine the first day's progress, we are distressed to discover that only two machines have been completed. Should we panic? Probably not.

The technician might have started the task by inspecting all sixty upgrade kits to ensure that each contained all of the correct supplies. In this case, the effort required on the remaining fifty-eight machines may be less than two hours per machine. In addition, it is possible that the machines are of different ages and configurations, and the technician may have decided to take the most difficult machines first, knowing that they would take more time per machine. There may be other machines in the queue that will take substantially less than two hours per machine. And it is possible that the technician spent seven hours on the first machine, figuring how to install and test the upgrade most efficiently. Having done so, the second machine may have only taken one hour, and the other fifty-eight machines may take less than one hour each because of the learning curve. There are a number of circumstances in which our linear extrapolation is misleading and distressful.

It is not a linear world, and therefore linear plans fail the project manager. More often than not, there is a nonlinear plan in the minds of those performing the work. If this is the case, you cannot afford to accept a linear plan from the members of the project team. In developing the project plan, communicate the desire for a nonlinear plan and facilitate the gathering of nonlinear plan data. The software used must be capable of accepting nonlinear data and using them as the basis for comparisons with actual performance.

The example we worked through for Activity ABC had an inherent assumption in it: the schedule called for the production of twenty units per week. It is often the case that there is a nonlinear baseline for the production of deliverables within a project or an activity. Let's make a different assumption and work through the activity again. There should be some dramatically different results.

### Example 2

Assume that the 100 units mentioned, at a cost of $75 each, are going to be produced according to the following schedule:

| Week | Units |
|------|-------|
| 1 | 10 |
| 2 | 15 |
| 3 | 20 |
| 4 | 25 |
| 5 | 30 |

This activity is scheduled to take 5 weeks, during which time 100 units are to be produced, each unit costing the firm $75. The status of this activity at the end of the third week is the same as in Example 1: 50 units have been produced earning the value (BCMP) of $3,750 (50 units × $75 per unit = $3,750) and $5,000 has been spent (ACMP).

## Questions

Answer the questions that follow concerning the status of this project and its forecast of projections.

1.  What should have been accomplished at the end of the third week: in other words, what is the plan?

    _____ units should have been produced.

    $_____ should have been spent (BCMS).

2.  The project's cost variance = BCMP − ACMP = _____

    Are we over or under budget? _____

3.  Schedule variance in cost terms = BCMP − BCMS = _____

    Are we ahead of or behind schedule? _____

4.  Cost performance index (CPI) = BCMP/ACMP = _____

    Are we performing better or worse than planned? _____

5.  Schedule performance index (SPI) (in $) = BCMP/BCMS = _____

    Are we performing better or worse than planned? _____

6.  Budgeted cost for remaining work = BAC − BCMP (where BAC = budget at completion) = _____

7.  Estimate to complete the project (ETC) = (BAC − BCMP)/CPI =

    _____

8.  Total estimate at completion (forecasted cost) (EAC) = ACMP + ETC = _____

## Answers

1.  The plan is to produce 45 units and to spend $3,375 (BCMS).
2.  The project's cost variance = BCMP − ACMP (determines whether the completed work has cost more or less than was budgeted for that work) = $3,750 − $5,000 = − $1,250.

    We are over budget.
3.  Schedule variance in dollars = BCMP − BCMS (compares work completed to work scheduled) = $3,750 − $3,375 = $375, or 5 units at $75 per unit.

    We are ahead of schedule.
4.  Cost performance index (CPI) = BCMP/ACMP = $3,750/$5,000 = 75 percent.

    Less than 100.0 indicates poor performance. We are performing worse than planned.

5. Schedule performance index (SPI) = BCMP/BCMS = \$3,750/ \$3,375 = 111 percent.
   Less than 100.0 indicates poor performance. We are performing better than planned.
6. Budgeted cost for remaining work = BAC − BCMP (where BAC = budget at completion) = \$7,500 − \$3,750 = \$3,750.
7. Estimate to complete the project (ETC) in dollars = (BAC − BCMP)/CPI = (\$7,500 − \$3,750)/.75 = \$5,000.
8. Total estimate at completion of project or the forecasted final cost (EAC) = ACMP + ETC = \$5,000 + \$5,000 = \$10,000.

Let's compare the answers we obtained from assuming the linear and nonlinear plans for the units to be produced.

| Item | Linear Plan | Nonlinear Plan |
| --- | --- | --- |
| Planned output | 60 | 45 |
| Actual output | 50 | 50 |
| Cost variance | +\$750 | −\$1,250 |
| Cost status | under | over |
| Schedule variance | −\$750 | +\$375 |
| Schedule status | behind | ahead |
| CPI | 125 percent | 75 percent |
| Cost performance | good | poor |
| SPI | 83.3 percent | 111 percent |
| Schedule performance | poor | good |
| Budget for remaining work | \$3,750 | \$3,750 |
| Estimate to complete | \$3,000 | \$5,000 |
| Estimate at completion | \$6,000 | \$10,000 |

Earned value is often analyzed graphically. Figure 9-3 shows the earned value plan using the nonlinear data from Example 2. The y-axis coordinates are the number of units (left side) and percentage complete (right side). Dollars could also be used as a y-axis. You might be concerned at the increasing pace of unit production which has been planned by the project team. Figure 9-4 is an example of the earned value plan (BCMS) and earned value actual (BCMP) for this activity at the end of the third week using the nonlinear data. It is quite clear that the effort is ahead of schedule. Figure 9-5 shows the earned value plan and earned value actual with actual cost data for the activity using the nonlinear data from Figures 9-3 and 9-4. The earned value actual (BCMP) is over the earned value plan (BCMS); therefore, the effort is ahead of schedule. However, the actual cost (ACMP) is well over the earned value plan (BCMS); therefore, the effort is substantially over budget.

Having these types of data makes it easier for you to check the information given to you by project team members or by their functional

(Text continues on page 171.)

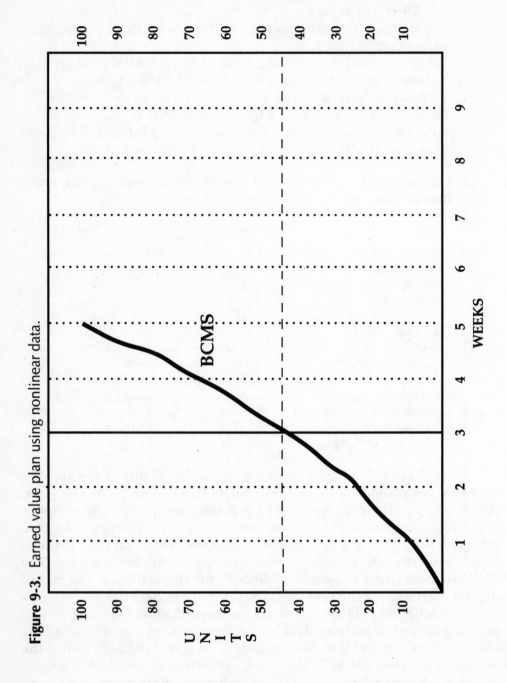

**Figure 9-3.** Earned value plan using nonlinear data.

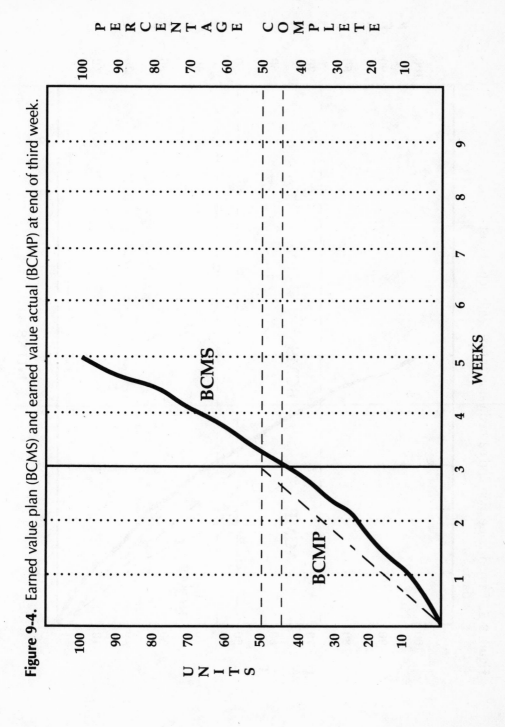

**Figure 9-4.** Earned value plan (BCMS) and earned value actual (BCMP) at end of third week.

**Figure 9-5.** Earned value plan and earned value actual, with actual cost data.

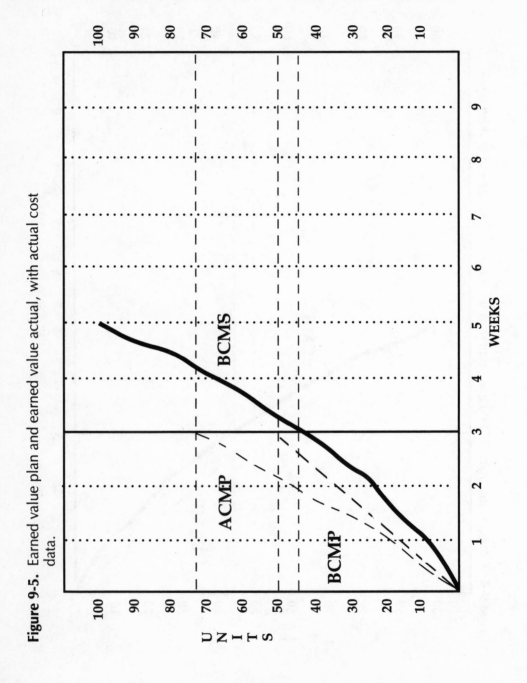

bosses. Measurements for earned value or work accomplishment have more substance and integrity than just schedule and cost variances and are a better base from which to extrapolate future costs and schedules. Incidentally, it is also true that the nonlinear relationships tend to prevail when looking at person-hours versus time, and therefore the nonlinear planning requirements apply to the measurement of actuals as well.

# Chapter 10

## Supporting Project Management: Software, Training, and Administration

In this chapter, we explore three of the many support issues relative to project management:

- *Software support:* Employing automated tools to manipulate project management data in order to plan, control, and investigate what-if simulations, and to generate meaningful reports.
- *Training support:* Teaching interested parties about the organization's project management methodology, their project management process and associated tool kit, and the chosen software tool (if one exists).
- *Administrative support:* Providing qualified help to the project manager and functional managers of the project team with the purpose of collecting, processing, and disseminating project management information.

Many companies appear to believe that once they purchase a piece of project management software, all of their project managers will become competent overnight. Buying a project management scheduling package does not ensure success, however. First, one must understand the basics of project management in order to prepare the data for system entry, comprehend the logic the software uses to calculate the output, and be able to interpret the data and request meaningful reports.

Training is required to provide a grounding in the fundamental tools and techniques of project management. In addition, the project manager and team members must be given the time to plan, monitor, and track the project—an effort that cannot be accomplished in one's spare time. If the project manager is not given the time to do the project management job correctly, administrative support must be found to take away some of the burden.

## Software Support

Choosing the right project management software package used to be as easy as going to a local computer store and seeing what was available, but accelerating changes in project management software have mandated a different approach. More emphasis on sophisticated features and ease of use require an in-depth evaluation of the major alternatives. The payoff is a more effective implementation of project management.

In 1955, the project management software count was zero. By 1981, it had increased to approximately 220. The number of products introduced to perform project management functions on the computer, mainframe or mini, was impressive. In the early 1980s project management software packages were introduced for the microcomputer. The functionality was very limited, yet this was the most significant step in the evolution of project management software in at least a decade.

Today over 1,300 new products are available to perform project management functions. Four hundred of these are microcomputer-based, MS-DOS machine-based products. How many will there be tomorrow? Clearly the answer is fewer. Certainly project management is an expanding market, and more and more organizations are realizing that a portion of their workload lends itself to being managed with project management, but the market is not broad enough to support that many products. There has to be a shakeout in the project management software business. Some companies and some products—including good ones—will not survive. This represents a risk to the organization acquiring a project management software product. Will the company be there to provide technical support? Will there be new releases, fixing bugs and/or offering new features desired by the customer base? If new, incompatible hardware product lines are introduced, will there be new releases of the software that will run on the hardware? All of these questions can be a major concern to the potential buyer. None of the answers is easy. The companies offering the products range in size from one-person operations to giants of industry. Neither may survive in the face of intense competition. Financial resources do not, in and of themselves, guarantee survival. The risk may not be capable of being managed, but certainly it must be recognized when the software decision is presented to management for approval.

Before you begin your search for the perfect package, do your homework. Conduct a thorough analysis of your current project management methodology to determine your specific requirements for a software package. Devise a comprehensive checklist of all the requirements necessary for you to manage your projects using a software tool. Describe the way you utilize resources, handle job costs and budgets, handle task assignments and task relationships, want to see reports, and so forth. On your checklist, note which items are mandatory, which are highly desirable, and which are window dressing. Once you have your checklist you're ready to evaluate products. But first, let's take a look at what project management software can and cannot do:

### What Project Management Software Can Do

- Perform calculations such as early start, early finish, late start, late finish, float, critical path, resource loading, and labor budget extrapolations, to name but a few.
- Allow you to try various scenarios to determine the impact of changes.
- Sort and extract data to produce a variety of reports.
- Perform some of the calculations to level your overloaded resources or to meet a mandated target date.
- Portray the actuals compared to the plan from data you have entered.

### What Project Management Software Cannot Do

- Define the project objectives.
- Develop the work breakdown structure.
- Determine the logical dependencies of tasks one to another.
- Choose who should be working on which tasks.
- Estimate the duration of tasks.
- Fix all the problems of resource overloading or attempt to meet a mandated target date by compressing the critical path.
- Design the correct reports for different people on your distribution list.

The bottom line is that project management software cannot do your thinking. What it can do is take the laborious work out of calculating and recalculating the data and out of preparing handwritten reports.

### *Defining Key Software Features*

The following features are of significance in evaluating the suitability of individual project management programs to your specific application.

### Pricing

There is only a slight correlation between price and performance. Some $500 products outperform products costing six to ten times as much. The fullest-featured products are not on the shelves of your local software store. With but a few exceptions, the products that have more functionality are marketed directly by the source to the end user. These products tend to be somewhat less well known and are more difficult to locate to include in a comparative evaluation. The products in the store may be sufficient to meet your needs, but if they are not, look further. Sales volume is not an indicator of quality or functionality. Many products have sold on the basis of their name or reputation, without having any significant feature advantage over less well-known products sitting unused on bookshelves. Features are being added at a frantic pace. Most vendors are working feverishly to add capabilities to their products, and the rate at which updates are being released is increasing.

### Number of Activities

What is the total number of activities (tasks) that may be assigned to any project—to both the main project and each subproject? We are witnessing a gradual evolution away from a strict numerical restriction toward the terms *limited by the system* or *unlimited*. You will need to investigate whether the number of activities is limited by the amount of available main memory in your computer or by disk capacity. Check the limiting factors and whether the capacities meet your minimum functional requirements.

### Total Resources

What are the total numbers of resources—individuals, skill categories, equipment categories, materials, and others—available for assignment at any given time? Some packages limit the number of resources per task; others limit the number per project. Determine what software factors limit resources and what your minimum constraints are before you purchase.

### Direct Costs

How does the software package handle direct costs (material, equipment, supplies) that may be assigned to each activity? If you want a detailed accounting, confirm that the categories may be both listed and accumulated by specific item rather than by a generic title such as "Fixed Costs" or "Other Costs." Consider how the costs are allocated: up front, amortized across the duration, in fixed payments, at specific performance milestones, or at the end of an activity—or whether you have a choice. The program's capability for allocating and reporting the respective direct costs by time periods is a significant feature.

### Resource Availability and Allocation

It is not realistic to expect that any one resource will be made available 100 percent of its time to a specific project. Resource availability and allocation features allow the planner to designate the number of hours a resource is available to the project and/or the percentage of the resource's time that is committed to the project. In more sophisticated packages, the resource allocation feature can provide overtime costing, lag starts of individual resources, multiple shift allocation, and individual resource calendars for scheduling vacations, holidays, and conferences.

### Resource-Constrained Scheduling

Where resources are overscheduled, resource leveling is employed. Tasks on noncritical paths are moved within their float and/or elongated into their float. This reduces the amount of resources required during any one unit of time. If the movement of tasks does not resolve the problem—in other words, some resources are still overscheduled—the critical path activities are delayed until no resource is scheduled more than the number of hours that it has available to the project. When the effect on the completion date is recalculated, the project may take longer than originally scheduled. Selective changes may then be made to task priorities, dependencies, resource assignments, and other alternatives to reach a balance between the original and extended completion dates. These changes may be repeated in an iterative fashion until a compromise acceptable to the project team and management is achieved. It is particularly important to allocate resources intelligently during the planning stages. Although the same results could be obtained by manually adjusting assignments and durations, it is more efficient and effective to have a computer system perform the calculations.

### On-Screen Network Diagram

An on-screen network representation of the activities and milestones in a project is an integral tool for successful project management. Systems that provide on-screen networks may permit activities to be moved on the screen to achieve an optimum presentation for report purposes. Other programs, in comparison, provide a fixed network diagram, which generally is the result of entries made in the task and/or Gantt screens.

### On-Screen Schedule/Gantt Chart

Planners require graphic schedule information, and most packages use the Gantt or bar chart format, which shows the activities on a time-scale orientation. Gantt charts display start, end, and durations of tasks within the project. This format is widely used as a planning, monitoring, and tracking device. Some products show the interfaces of predecessor(s) to successor(s); some do not.

### On-Screen Resource Utilization

On-screen presentation of how and when resources are utilized throughout the duration of the project is helpful to project managers. Presentation in some cases is displayed not only in tabular form but also in a graphic form, such as histograms. There may also be a capability to compare resource utilization with the activities to which the resource is assigned, sometimes on the same screen. Absence of this feature makes resolution of resource conflict much more difficult than it needs to be.

### Resource Leveling Within Float

When one or more resources is overloaded or overutilized, some effort must be made to relieve the situation. This is called leveling. Through an automatic option or manual intervention, this feature allows two options: (1) movement of noncritical tasks within float to resolve overloading or (2) the addition of qualified personnel or other resources. Consequently, this kind of leveling does not affect the scheduled completion date. Most current packages have a resource leveling option; however, they level by delaying tasks within float (option 1) only. They will not locate and utilize alternate resources of comparable skill that are underutilized and make a substitution. However, the product allows the project manager to accomplish this through menu-driven entries.

### Work Breakdown Levels

This is the number of levels to which project work can be broken down and reflected by the project management package. Generally detailed planning for task and resource assignment is done at the lowest level of detail and then rolled up to selected intermediate or top levels. For example, the highest levels may be feasibility phase, preliminary design phase, detailed design phase, development phase, and implementation phase. Feasibility can then be broken down into market analysis, needs analysis, and current system study, and market analysis may then be broken into telephone survey of Fortune 500 firms and competition survey. How many levels of detail and how well the system consolidates those levels is important to the planner. This person plans and manages at the lowest level but often reports at the higher levels.

### Tracking Schedule Progress

Recording the actual start time and duration for each activity, as well as the finish date, permits the planner to track the project. An additional feature is the ability to forecast the revised completion date based on the slippage during the earlier activities of the project.

### Tracking Budget Expenditures

The ability to record the actual costs (which often deviate from the plan) incurred during the progress of the project is an important feature of tracking. A project manager must be able to add current actual costs to update existing actual costs and produce reports documenting the planned and actual expenditures.

### Simulations

The capacity to perform a series of what-ifs (simulations of alternative options) iteratively is an effective option if the various alternative scenarios may be examined individually, saved to disk, and then compared with the original baseline plan. Effective project managers recognize the need for varied contingency plans, as well as the need to replan frequently according to circumstances.

### Calendar Flexibility

Software users may need to plan in intervals ranging from hours to months. Small projects may be planned in hours or days, whereas larger projects may be planned in weeks and months. Decide what units of time you need, from lowest to highest. Also decide if you need a combination of intervals in one project or when comparing multiple projects.

### Resource Calendars

You may need the ability to create unique calendars for each resource with varying workweeks, shifts, holidays, and/or shutdowns. Each of the individual resource calendars can be adjusted independently to accommodate a particular individual's availability. Some programs allow a calendar for each resource, especially helpful if personnel have different amounts of time available or you must schedule computer time, equipment time, or a subcontractor's time.

### Number of Subprojects

This capability allows you to create two or more subprojects linked to tasks in the main project. The details of the subprojects may be rolled up and summarized in the main project. Any change in network scheduling affecting the parent task will be reflected in the subproject, and vice versa.

### Multiproject Resource Allocation

This feature is critical in an environment where individual and group resources are assigned to several concurrent projects. Projects sharing common resources need to be reviewed as a group in order to examine the aggregate resource utilization and costs over particular time periods. Multiproject composite resource allocation tables are useful to point out both overloading and underutilization of resources and to facilitate their reassignment, change task relationships, or other actions to accomplish resource leveling.

### Cost and Budget Documentation

A comprehensive project management software package must be able to create or accept baseline budget data and actual costs and create comparative reports. The reports should be available in tabular and graph format identifying variances for specific resources, activities, or categories of costs. Although planners may not place a lot of weight on this feature, most managers will.

### Report Generator

A good software package will provide you with the capability to prepare standard and special reports. Many standard report formats do not meet specific needs. The addition of a report generator to customize output allows timely creation of meaningful output and greatly expands the utility of a program.

### Graphics/Plotter

Newer programs support an increasing number of attractively priced plotters. Some programs, however, require the purchase of a supplemental piece of software to accomplish this end. The addition of a plotter or plotter-quality printer allows you to create presentation-quality output, as well as large-size document for project displays.

### Data Export

A common means of performing detailed analysis on project data not available within a project management package is to export data to other programs. A project management software program should accomplish all of the primary and essential planning activities. Some allow export of project data to other types of programs that perform auxiliary tasks. Spread sheets, database, and graphic display packages are more appropriate for certain jobs, and the easy transfer of data makes this interface particularly attractive.

### Windows

Windows permit the simultaneous presentation of two or more program displays on screen, such as Gantt charts and resource histograms. Such dual displays allow you to compare cause and effect without continually switching from one display to another.

### Micro/Mainframe Connection

The availability of software to accommodate transfer of data between the micro-based software and the mainframe environments can be invaluable. This option offers the ability to transfer data from the personal computer(s) to the mainframe (and vice versa) and permits the accumulation, manipulation, and reporting of companywide information on a compatible mainframe project management package. This migration of data to the mainframe also allows multiuser access to project management data. There may be a further interface of these data into accounting, inventory, or purchasing systems.

### Vendor Support

The vendor or publisher should provide some or all of the following: training, installation, maintenance and updates, and hot-line support. Updates are supplied free of charge within a certain period from purchase or at a per-copy fee. It is important to explore the vendor's customer support services before you purchase a system. Verify that there is a telephone number and responsive staff to answer questions.

### User Manual

This document must provide a well-organized, broad coverage of the program's features, with a complete index. A well-written manual facilitates the learning process, explains clearly the full features of the program, and provides quick access to sections relating to specific problems. The quality of a user manual can be judged by the speed with which needed information can be quickly located and understood.

Choosing the right software program can be an expensive and time-consuming process. For those of you who have had to live with a less-than-perfect choice and for those of you who wish to avoid one, the time and money is well spent. If you are in the process of choosing software, consider using the following seven-step process.

1. Work with the people who will be using the product and decide on the features you require and those that you would like.
2. Obtain some literature on project management. The Project Management Institute in Drexel Hill, Pennsylvania, has a directory, and PC magazines often publish articles comparing products. Another alternative is to ask around.
3. Pick several products that will satisfy your specifications.
4. Acquire demonstration versions of the products you have decided will fit your needs.
5. Conduct benchmark tests against each product's demonstration package. Set up a small project that typifies the data in your organization. Run the data through each of the products to determine if the product meets your criteria. In general, evaluate the products for ease of data entry, what-if simulations, entering actual data and extracting reports and management roll-ups of data, quality of screen and report presentation, multiple project analysis (if this is one of your criteria), and processing volumes of data. Reproduce your benchmark test data to equal the maximum transactions you will want to process. Run this mass of data through several functions of the product and see if the processing speed slows down.
6. Now that you have made your choice, send out a public relations memo explaining your expectations with this new software. Then provide training on the basics of project management (if necessary) and on the product, and offer some assistance to those trying to get up to speed. You may want to be their in-house hot-line.
7. Demonstrate to the project team and to management that you intend to maintain the discipline required to use this product. The minute you relax the requirements for plans or status reports from the project management scheduling, almost everyone will drop the software like a hot potato. If you keep the energy and urgency high, you can expect support.

## Current Trends

### Speed

New releases are being reworked to increase the speed of processing. In some cases, only certain features of the product have speed increases; in others, all of the system's processing is being accelerated. The speed increases range from barely discernible to dramatic; certain products tout increases of close to 1,000 percent on many functions. Some products are now pushing the speed limitations of the hardware, yet there is room for further improvements in speed through hardware upgrades. As chip-based machines proliferate in the businss community, dramatic speed increases in all microcomputer-based project management products will be experienced.

### Work Breakdown Structure Support

More software vendors are coming to realize the critical role of the work breakdown structure in project management and are including support for WBS in their products. Some are including the ability to print or plot the WBS diagram among the features of their new releases.

### Increased Capacity

Many vendors are increasing the capacity of their products, typically in tasks per project, resources per database, resources per task, predecessors per task, and direct costs per task. Even memory-based products (the project must be resident in memory while being worked upon) are increasing their capacity by taking advantage of memory above the 640K limitation on MS-DOS microcomputers. Because of increased capacity, field sizes are being increased, allowing more flexibility, especially for adding narrative comments.

### More Resource Functions

This may be the area in which the most significant improvements are being made. The new features that are surfacing in some products include the ability to make nonlinear resource assignments within a task, so that an individual can work on a ten-day task for four hours per day the first week and eight hours per day the second week. More products are including resource-constrained scheduling capabilities, so that the demand for resources can be reduced to the capacity of the organization, at the expense of the end date of the project. The algorithms used for resource-constrained scheduling are improving. They take the critical path into account and minimize the delay in the project while leveling the demand for resources. Many products are adding resource leveling (within float) capabilities to the system. Unlike resource-constrained scheduling, resource leveling does not allow the project end date to change and often yields imperfect leveling results. The algorithms for resource leveling are also improving; many can now factor a user-determined task priority into the calculations. Some systems now allow the assignment of resources in hours, days, weeks, or months, all within the same project. Many products are addressing the need to alter the cost of resources on a time-scaled basis. It is now possible to vary the hourly rate of a resource either annually or by establishing "from" and "to" dates for the rates. The number of resources allowed per task and per database has been increasing. The use of different calendars for each resource is becoming more popular. The major advantage to the resource calendar approach is that it allows the organization to track and to factor into project schedules planned training, vacations, and other administrative time. Finally, ability to use PERT (Program Evaluation Review Technique) and earned value calculations is becoming available.

### Scheduling Flexibility

Many systems have limited the user to input of durations in one standard unit per project. Thus, prior to data entry, the user had to decide to enter all durations in hours, days, weeks, or months. Once the decision was made, it could not be changed. An increasing number of systems now allow the time units to be determined at the task level rather than at the project level. Thus, Task A can be entered with a duration of forty hours, and Task B can be entered with a duration of three weeks. In some older systems, only durations entered in days were allowed if holidays were to be factored into the schedule calculations. Holidays were ignored if durations were entered in weeks or months. Increasingly that is no longer the case. Holidays are now recognized regardless of the units used for entry of durations.

### Better Reporting

In systems that lack report writers, a more impressive menu of standard reports is becoming available. Although there is still a lack of flexibility in this feature, the end user is more likely to find what is desired in the expanded menu of reports. The report writers are also becoming more flexible, allowing users a wider range of choices in structuring personalized reports. One annoying characteristic of the older report writers is gradually disappearing. In many older systems, the personalized report had to be recreated each time it was run; there was no provision to save the report so that it could be rerun periodically. More systems are now allowing the user to save the personalized report and to recall and rerun it as required. A few menu-driven systems even allow the user to place the personalized report name in the menu of reports.

### Ease of Data Entry

Many systems are adding features that can reduce the amount of time and effort required to get the project data into the system. Screens on which multiple tasks can be entered are one result of this improvement. Copy, paste, and combine functions are another. The user can now create a group of repeating tasks and copy them as many times as required in building the plan. If there are ten tasks to the design of a circuit board, for example, and nine circuit boards to be designed, ten entries (rather than ninety) are required. The combine function allows models to be built and then used in many projects.

### Output Device Support

The range of printers and plotters supported by the software is increasing dramatically. Larger and faster printers and plotters are now being supported, even by microcomputer-based products. This gives an acceptable output speed to the product, even when very large projects are being reported upon.

### System Linkages

There is an increasing trend for smaller, easier-to-use products to provide uploading facilities to more capable systems. This allows the plan to be built in an interactive mode on a small, very user-friendly system and the status reports to be generated on a larger, more complex, and full-featured project management system.

Project management software vendors are becoming more responsive to the user community. When the first microcomputer-based products were introduced, people bought them because there was little choice, and some functionality was better than none. Today, with a broad range of choices for the end user, a more responsive approach is required. The future will continue to bring greater functionality and increased speed.

## Training Support

With or withour project management software, training support positions a project organization for success. Training is not a one-time effort. It should be planned on an annual basis. There is new information to learn relative to the tools of the trade and relative to how to work in project organizations. Moreover, new staff who join the project team need to be brought up to speed.

This section looks at two relatively new modes of training, both reliant on computer support: a self-paced, independent study training approach called computer-based training or (CBT) and a classroom training technique called computer simulation training. We also discuss an older approach, on-the-job training, a technique that is not being used as frequently as it might.

### Computer-Based Training

Computer-based training (CBT) is an automated version of programmed instruction. This type of training consists of text that presents a problem to which the student provides an answer. Then the student refers to the solution to determine whether he or she has the correct answer. The problem may be in the form of multiple choice questions, fill-in-the-blanks, mathematical problems, or charts or graphs to be drawn.

CBT presents these problems on a computer screen. The student responds via the keyboard. The software not only validates the answer with approval or disapproval, but the response is specific relative to the student's answer, provides guidance and rationale as to why the answer was wrong, and describes what constitutes a correct answer.

The most effective project management CBT products are those that are accompanied by an interactive workbook. The software enables students to survey the subject, identify the key points, and do a minimal amount of practice. The interactive workbook encourages students to practice the new skill using paper and pencil until they become facile with the technique. The workbook presents a case study from beginning to end to enable students to visualize and develop a perspective of how the tools integrate with one another. Furthermore, the workbook can allow students to explore subjects in greater depth than is covered in the software.

The combined power of the CBT software and the workbook provides diversity in training modes, variation of pace in training activities, and changes in perspective, all designed to keep the student stimulated.

CBT is not intended to replace classroom training. The classroom provides a forum for exploration of ideas, for presenting questions and problems, and for communicating with others of similar backgrounds; CBT is designed as a primer before going into a classroom setting, as a reinforcement after a seminar is completed, or as a stop-gap training for a new project team member until the next seminar is scheduled.

CBT was not created with the goal of being completed at a single session; users set their own pace. A novice user may want to work systematically through each part of the package in sequence, whereas more advanced users may want to review selected sections. This flexibility in the training tool allows students to access specific functions within project management to support individual needs and growth.

### Computer-Based Simulation Training

This mode of training simulates risks in the environment as a means to stimulate creative solutions and produce high-quality results. Simulation-type training has been used for centuries in a classroom with teams such as the military, to teach tactics and strategies to use in combat. Alternative scenarios were presented to the students; the students responded, and their choices were classified as successful or unsuccessful. The students benefited by learning from their failures and being reinforced by their successes.

Flight simulators facilitate trainee pilots' learning the controls and the proper responses during varied flight conditions without risking their lives or the lives of others. After World War II, Monopoly was used to teach returning veterans how to operate in the real estate industry without risking any of their capital.

Simulation training is employing a case study approach. Traditionally, a case is presented to the student in a classroom, the student responds, and the response is classified as successful or unsuccessful. There are two drawbacks with this type of case study training: the evaluations of success or failure are often subjective and dependent on the instructor or fellow team members, and no matter what the student's response is, the case study itself is not dynamic, and change is not in response to the choices of the student.

Computer-based simulation training introduces an element of reality to the case study. Since the computer is driven by dynamic software, its response is dependent on the input. That response is fast paced and encourages the student to move quickly from scenario to scenario and from learning experience to learning experience. There is no delay while the instructor reconfigures the case or the team members critique the action taken.

In computer-based project management simulation training, the participant develops an initial plan and enters the schedule, resource assignments, and budget into the system. The software is not a project management scheduling system; it is not a programmed-instruction computer-based training; it is not a game. The software presents alternative scenarios to the participant, the participant responds, and his or her actions are graded as either successful or unsuccessful by the successive actions of the simulation and its output status reports. The participants are reinforced by their successes and learn from their failures.

The case thus transforms schedule, resources (both internal and external), and costs into conflict situations. All the classic project management charts and graphs are utilized. The participant is confronted with all the decision situations found in a project management environment. For example, during the simulation, project team members may quit, the equipment may malfunction, and contractors may not be productive. We say *may* because each team goes through its own unique labyrinth of situations when actual versus plan data are presented. Many months of project evolution are consolidated into a three- or four-day classroom experience, and each team follows a very different scenario.

Simulation training creates a classroom environment in which the members of the teams are closely united. Their one goal is to win. They win not by beating out the other teams (although competition can be felt within the room) but by meeting their original commitments: schedule, budget, morale of their team members, and quality. They are competing with themselves to do the best that they can. In order to accomplish this, the team must be able to reach consensus, be efficient in the assignment of roles within the group, and, most important, be proactive rather than reactive.

There are few project management computer-based simulation products on the market. One that we are familiar with offers two versions of project management simulations. The first addresses a single environment; the second, a multiproject scenario within a matrixed environment. The multiproject simulation assigns to each of the team members the role of one of three project managers or one of two functional managers. Single-project and multiproject management are very different and need to be positioned from different perspectives.

Computer-based simulations provide an exciting environment: lecture, team practice, dynamic feedback, baseline analysis, and, most important, real-world application embedded in the learning process. Project management simulation training is designed for those who say, "I've seen it all. I've been to project management seminars before. If there is something new, something beyond the basics, I'd be willing to go to another program. But until then, I'd be bored." Our experience indicates that those attending a simulation course are highly stimulated. Attendees have requested that the classroom be opened earlier than scheduled each morning and on the last day have negotiated with the instructor to keep the machines active "for just another half-hour."

### On-the-Job Training

What is on-the-job training in project management? Why is it needed, how does it work, and what are its benefits? Classroom training in project management has been the standard since the 1960s. It is a fine vehicle for presenting the concepts of project management, dealing with organizational issues, and establishing the mind-set necessary to plan and control work effort. Computer-based training has taken a place in the development of skills in scheduling, resource-cost planning, and control data processing. But neither classroom training nor computer-based training equips the new or potential project manager with the experience necessary to deal with projects and their problems on a daily basis. Even simulation-based training, which comes close to replicating the real world, does not have the pressure, sense of urgency, and sense of criticality that is present in real-world project management. None of the formal training vehicles fosters the long-term development of a project management style on the part of personnel being trained. Short of trial by fire, there is only one other alternative: on-the-job training.

On-the-job training in project management involves pairing an experienced project manager with a prospect to expose the new manager to behavioral patterns, style, and methods that yield effective planning and control of the work. It also can pair a new project manager with a project management consultant for the same purposes.

If the project manager in training is paired with a more senior project manager, there are two modes in which the training experience can be structured: (1) the more experienced project manager as the project manager of record or (2) the candidate as the project manager of record. We believe that the manager in training should be the manager of record. This yields a more meaningful training experience and allows for termination of the training when management has concluded that the objectives of the learning experience have been attained.

When the project manager in training is paired with a consultant, it is essential that the trainee be the project manager of record. In principle, we are opposed to the concept of an individual who is not an employee of the organization managing the project and giving direction to project team members who are employees of the organization. In addition, this is a costly method, and it will be of relatively short duration. Upon termination of the training experience, the project manager in training will continue to manage the project.

The most significant disadvantage of on-the-job training is cost. In absolute terms, it is expensive. Two salaries rather than one are applied to the management of the effort. Even if the training period is much shorter than the duration of the project, the costs will be significant. On the other hand, the costs pale in comparison to the potential cost to the organization of the trial-by-fire approach. The risk associated with trial by fire may serve to make the relatively modest cost of on-the-job training palatable to management.

A second disadvantage of on-the-job training is the possible transfer of bad habits and behaviors along with a transfer of desired habits and behaviors. This potential disadvantage can be overcome by extremely careful selection of the mentors, whether staff members or consultants, and by frequent monitoring and assessment of the transfer of knowledge.

Another drawback, which is related to the issue of cost, is the scarcity of project managers in the organization. The workload beckons, and anyone with the potential of performing the project management function may be conscripted to staff the backlog. Therefore, on-the-job training is best accomplished during periods of relatively slack demand, when the sense of urgency in staffing the workload is less pressing.

Advantages of on-the-job training are primarily contextual. It is the only means short of trial by fire of exposing the trainee to the actual project management environment, with all the variables that affect the project management processes and decision making in that environment. The project manager who has been through on-the-job training is potentially better equipped to undertake larger, more complex project assignments than the organization would trust to a new project manager who has not been through the process.

On-the-job training requires more than a management decision to undertake the effort and the selection of a mentor. It requires a plan, learning objectives, and periodic reviews of lessons learned, with a facilitator other than the new project manager's mentor.

In planning this experience, considerable attention should be given to the selection of the project. It should not be contrived, overly simple, or overly complex. In selecting the mentor, consideration should be given to the technical knowledge of both the mentor and the trainee. On-the-job training works best when both mentor and trainee have similar fields of technical experience. This creates a stronger bond between two people who will be spending a great number of hours together over a short period of time.

Finally, planning of the experience should include a schedule plan, with a target date for completion of the learning experience substantially in advance of the completion of the project. An initial decision should be made as to whether the mentor or the trainee will assume exclusive responsibility for the project at the end of the training period.

There should also be periodic reviews between the trainee and a third-party facilitator of any learning progress made. This facilitator could be the head of project management or another experienced project manager.

On-the-job training is costly, effective, time-consuming, and difficult with regard to a commitment of resources, but its potential benefit to the organization makes it worth considering as part of the total development plan for project managers.

### Administrative Support

Administrative support within an organization that uses project management optimizes the use of time by the project manager and the project team. The administrative support unit can be the custodian of the organization's project management standards. It can issue copies of the standards to all personnel requiring them; edit, produce, and distribute updates to the standards; and coordinate the process of modifying the standards, as required. This function clearly needs to be performed and does not require the attention of project managers.

The administrative support unit can be the point of contact between the organization and its project management software vendor. The unit manages the availability of the software for the staff. When new releases of the software become available, this unit coordinates the evaluation of the upgrade, installs new releases, provides training for the staff in the use of the software, and receives questions about the software.

When significant amounts of plan data have to be entered into the project management system, project managers should be able to request data entry support from this group. The group either has data entry resources or manages work flow to the data entry unit. In addition, this unit can manage the interface between the organization's project management software and its cost accounting and time reporting systems by periodically transferring cost and person-hour data into the project management system for status reporting purposes. Error checking, resolution of data problems, and reconciliation of incorrect project charges can all be handled by this unit.

While project managers and teams tend to produce their own reports from the project management system, the administrative support unit is responsible for the production of periodic multiproject reports. Monthly senior management summary status reports are requested, printed, and distributed by the unit. Multiproject resource reports, directed to functional (skill group) managers, are also produced by this unit. These responsibilities require the unit to ensure that all projects have been updated prior to generating the multiproject reports.

Finally, the administrative support unit can function as the project management archivist for the organization. Information concerning completed or current projects can often be utilized again by the organization. When such information is required, the unit can make the information available to the project manager and team. Among the items that can be archived are work breakdown structure models for projects, phases, or groups of tasks commonly performed in many projects; network models; historical estimates; and actual costs for standard tasks.

An administrative support function allows project managers more time to devote to their projects. The clerical work will be performed by clerical workers rather than managers. Specialists will devote their time to the organization's system interfaces rather than having each project manager attempt to deal with these complex interfaces. The bottom line is that each project manager, having been freed from the administrative burdens, can manage an additional portion of the workload. Thus, fewer project managers can control the workload of the organization.

One final word of caution is required: If an administrative support function is relied upon by senior management for an early warning reporting of project problems, the entire perception of the group in the organization changes. Project and function managers will no longer consider the group to be their service. The group will be regarded as an audit function, and its services will be utilized only with great reluctance. Project problems should be brought to the attention of senior management by the managers of the projects which are experiencing them, not by a support unit.

## Political Aspects of Support

The three mechanisms that can support project management—software support, training support, and administrative support—have technical and political aspects too.

The technical aspect of software support consists of the tangible software and the procedures that accompany it. There are political issues here as well. Should one software product be chosen for all people within the organization, or should each person (or group) be allowed to choose individually? There are arguments for both sides. Those who suggest individual software choices argue that different groups need different types of software support, and therefore each group should be allowed to pick a product fitting its own needs. On the other hand, if everyone picks software, how will the data ever be consolidated in a manner that will allow the management of the whole rather than fragmented pieces, and how will management ever be able to see a composite picture of the status, staffing, and expenditures of all the projects in the organization? We believe that most project management software products are competitive. If a product fits the basic requirements, then all groups should be willing to use it for the good of the overall organization.

Training also has technical and political aspects. Technically, the course material must be designed, training manuals developed, and qualified trainers brought up to speed. Politically, training is not always seen with a tangible return on investment. Whether the course is developed inside the organization or an outside training consultant is brought in, there is expense. And taking employees off their job to attend a training class is another expense. Therefore, management and the participants must be convinced that there is a meaningful reward in improved productivity and better efficiency for this expenditure of time and dollars.

Administrative support is less controversial but equally affected by both technical and political issues. Technically, a job position must be created for an administrative support person, a salary justified, and a job description developed. Politically, it may be difficult to convince management that an administrative support person is necessary. What is the project leader doing if most of his or her work is being done by the administrator? Are we paying two salaries to get one job done? The answer is "no." The administrator can offload some of the more detailed work from the project manager, who then has more time to work on managing the project. The other political issue is who is the right person to take this job. It is more than a clerical job. It requires some business knowledge and a strong logical bent, especially for checking the data for reasonability. It is also not the project manager's job, and the administrator will have to subvert his or her ambition to be the boss, at least while on this job. You as project manager may promise the administrator that this is an interim step in his or her career and there will be a promotion in a year or two. Even a year or two with a good administrator is worth the investment, and you will see how much this person lightens your load and allows you to concentrate on planning, problem isolation, and resolution.

# Index